About the Author

In 2016, Shakaila Forbes-Bell became the first Black person to earn a master's degree in psychology for fashion professionals at the London College of Fashion. Her research interrogated the under-representation of Black models in fashion media, its impact on consumer behaviour and the self-concept of young Black women. After her paper was published in the *International Journal of Market Research*, she created the platform 'Fashion is Psychology' and has worked with global brands to unpack the psychological impact of style and beauty.

Shakaila's insights have been featured in publications including *Vogue, Forbes, Harper's Bazaar, The Guardian, Marie Claire, Stylist, Grazia* and more. She is regularly called on to comment on trends, sustainability research and representation in the fashion industry, and has provided psychologically focused PR, branding and market-ing advice to international brands including Maybelline, Next and Afterpay. *Big Dress Energy* is her first book. She lives in London.

Shakaila
Forbes–Bell

BIG
DRESS
ENERGY

How Fashion Psychology Can
Transform Your Wardrobe
and Your Confidence

PIATKUS

PIATKUS

First published in Great Britain in 2022 by Piatkus

1 3 5 7 9 10 8 6 4 2

A CIP catalogue record for this book
is available from the British Library.

ISBN 978-0-3494-3184-0

Typeset in Sabon by M Rules
Printed and bound in Great Britain by TJ Books Ltd, Padstow, Cornwall

Papers used by Piatkus are from well-managed forests
and other responsible sources.

FSC
www.fsc.org

MIX
Paper from
responsible sources
FSC® C013056

Piatkus
An imprint of
Little, Brown Book Group
Carmelite House
50 Victoria Embankment
London EC4Y 0DZ

An Hachette UK Company
www.hachette.co.uk

www.littlebrown.co.uk

This book is dedicated to my darling sister, Janelle.
In my heart forever, until we can laugh again together.

Contents

A note to readers

Big Dress Energy is all about giving you the tools to develop a stronger relationship with your clothes. For too long, these insights have been confined to stuffy academic papers that most people can't read for lack of access – and also because, well, they can be kind of boring. Between the Beyoncé references and nods to *The Real Housewives* franchise, I've made this research accessible, fun and useful. If you want to be empowered with science-based tips on how to curate a mindful wardrobe, let go of harmful shopping habits, and only wear clothes that speak to who you are at your core, then this is the book for you.

Introduction

What on earth is fashion psychology?

Ten years ago, I didn't have a bloody clue what fashion psychology was either. Now, I honestly consider it essential for the well-being of anyone who wears clothes – and since leaving your house with your bits out is considered a bit of a faux pas these days, that basically means everybody. This book isn't your run-of-the-mill style guide. Don't expect to learn a bunch of rules about which accessories give *French girl chic* vibes or how mixing navy and black is some sort of cardinal sin. This is not that. It's the culmination of a decade of research, two degrees, and a lot of groundwork, and my aim is to give you the ultimate guide to rewiring your brain so that you can embrace a healthier relationship with your wardrobe (and, hopefully, I'll make you laugh along the way too).

Nothing gives me more satisfaction than watching the cloud of confusion clear from someone's face as I explain what fashion psychology really is. Their frown softens, their eyes widen, and, if you're really quiet, you can hear bells ringing in their head as they eagerly nod along. Most people have a basic understanding of fashion psychology. You know that if you dress good, you feel good and that it's possible to power-dress your way into bigger rooms and better conversations. But for most people, the knowledge stops there, which crushes me. It's frustrating because a good deal of the quality research I've included in this book isn't new. It's simply been kept just out of reach. The sheer brainpower it takes to decipher what's actually being said in some of these academic papers is enough to make you fall asleep, but I've done all of the tedious work, so you don't have to. Allow me to break it down. In a nutshell, fashion psychology is:

- the way your clothes allow you to navigate different versions of yourself
- the reasons why you buy the things you do
- the way your clothes change not only your mood but how you think and behave
- the way clothes impact your body image
- the way people use their style to define themselves and others

When I graduated in 2016, I became the first Black woman to earn a master's degree in psychology for fashion professionals. My graduation picture, in which I'm wearing a sickening (if I do say so myself) black French Connection dress and proudly waving a singular fist up high, went viral. I managed to stay on cloud nine for about five seconds after that happened, because that's how long it took for the trolls to descend. Between comments like 'You're going to end up working at McDonald's' and 'Good luck paying off those student loans', I gathered that the general attitude of the nay-sayers was that it's stupid to care about clothes that much. But I'll tell you what the OG of fashion psychology, psychologist and award-winning author Michael Solomon told me: 'It can't be trivial because it pertains to what we're all doing.' Michael's right. It doesn't matter if you work in luxury fashion or construction – fashion and style are neither beneath nor above you. Even if you claim to put very little thought into your wardrobe, the truth is that just by buying clothes, choosing how to wear them and getting dressed in the morning, you've become an active participant in the process of fashion.

We often think of our clothes as possessions separate from ourselves, when in reality they act as a second skin. The most crucial power your clothes possess is the ability to help you lean in to who you truly are in a way that's bigger than 'you are what you wear'. Costume designer Cobbie Yates, who's worked on sets for TV shows like *The Fear Index* and movies like *Pirates*, told me: 'A well thought-out style starts with an understanding of yourself.' I couldn't agree more. Most style tips are based on rigid dos and don'ts that align to a specific stylistic viewpoint or aesthetic that doesn't give room for self-expression. Throughout this book, I've included fashion psychology tips based on scientific research to help you use your personal style to embody both yourself and your *self* – your essential being, the thing that differentiates you from other people.

If you zoom out a bit and look at what's going on in fashion right now, you'll see a paradox. People want more from their clothes. They want their clothes to look good, feel good, help them belong and at the same time be functional. They want their clothes to be ethical and sustainable, but at the same time, they simply want *more* clothes. How easy is it to drown out those videos featuring heaving piles of clothing waste with the knock-knock-knock of a delivery driver ready to lift your spirits with a new pair of jeans? And how come you have enough clothes to dress a small village and still have nothing to wear? For too long, fashion psychology has been missing from the equation. I'm not trying to vilify people for loving clothes, because I love them too, and I'm not here to paint brands and retailers as comic book villains – although I can't lie, they do have a couple of tricks up their sleeves. From the moment we set foot in a shop, click on a webpage or tap on a screen, we're bombarded with psychological tactics. These tactics make it incredibly tricky to shop smart, but it is possible – and it's easier to do when you know your stuff. When you think about it, curating a wardrobe or a look that you're proud of is simply a matter of making the right decisions. Sure, it may be easier said than done, but psychological studies have proven that it's all about carefully weighing your options, asking yourself the right questions and checking in with your mental and emotional processes.[1] This book shows you how to do just that.

I would be remiss if I didn't acknowledge that your personal style extends beyond your clothes. I've always been the cousin who turns up to small family gatherings with a full face of make-up and gets asked, 'Why are you doing the most?'. I've always considered experimenting with my appearance, no matter the occasion, to be a profoundly moving experience, and research in beauty psychology supports that. The way your skincare routine doubles as a legitimate form of self-care, how your make-up channels your creativity, and how your hair is inextricably tied to your identity means anything you do to maintain these parts of yourself could never be 'too much'.

I didn't just wake up one day and think, 'Hmm, let me pick a degree that almost no one has heard of. Yeah, that'll be easy.' You don't exactly see 'fashion psychologist' vacancies posted on LinkedIn job boards, but my love of clothes, hair and beauty ran too deep for me to not give it a try. Growing up, I wanted to be a dancer. I learned the routine of every dance break from the early 2000s, but my body couldn't keep up with the boom-kaks the other girls were hitting. When I got my first sewing machine, I wanted to be a fashion designer, but I broke my needle too many times and quickly lost patience. After I got a ninety-eight in my A level psychology exam, I decided I would become the Black female

Frasier; those were my exact words. Still, the reality of a career in clinical psychology knocked me on my ass when I got to university.

Not willing to give up on my love of fashion, I used my social psychology class as an opportunity to explore my hunch about the impact of clothing on our cognitive functioning – and I was blown away. So, I started the blog *Fashion is Psychology*, got an internship with a kick-ass style psychologist (hey, Kate!), and found a sympathetic advisor in Professor Adrian Furnham, who gave me the grace to write an entire dissertation about the intersection between race, hoodies and first impressions.

As if by design, a random Google search during a post-graduation existential crisis led me to a master's course in psychology for fashion professionals at the London College of Fashion. I was hesitant at first, but I applied after the third 'You're stupid if you don't do this' from my mother and sister. If you're unfamiliar with fashion schools, I'll paint you a picture. Luxury labels are the norm, and people are so well put-together they could easily be mistaken for runway models. Then picture me, a broke twenty-one-year-old psychology geek who watched *Coronation Street*, was always trying to discuss the latest Soca song and could barely tell her McCartneys from her McQueens.

On top of that, I was the only Black person on my course, and one of the few Black faces walking around the entire campus. Talk about a fish out of water. When I say this book is for everyone, I mean it, because I know what it's like to be excluded from the conversation and to feel like great style is only possible for a certain type of person. The more I researched, the more I realised that great style doesn't look one way – and it's certainly not found in a price tag.

Measuring your Big Dress Energy

Let's get into this title. I know it's giving 'no one knows what it means, but it's provocative', but I promise you there's a method to the madness. Before I delve into the explanation, I've crafted a handy quiz to help you determine how much Big Dress Energy you have right now.

The big 'Big Dress Energy' quiz

For each statement below, give yourself a score from one to seven, with one being 'strongly disagree' and seven being 'strongly agree'.

		Strongly disagree						Strongly agree
	Score	1	2	3	4	5	6	7
1	What I wear is often consistent with who I am.							
2	I sometimes use my wardrobe to help me become the person I want to be.							
3	I use clothes and accessories to help me express or manage my emotions.							
4	I wear different styles to reflect different parts of my identity.							
5	I often wear certain clothing to let people know what kind of person I am.							
6	I want my clothes and accessories to make a statement about me without any need for words.							
7	I'm aware of the impression my personal style gives off.							
8	I know how to control the way I'm perceived through my style.							
9	I'm aware of how my behaviour changes when I wear different outfits.							

10	I use clothes and accessories to help me navigate different social situations.							
11	I'm careful about buying from certain retailers because I want them to align with my personal beliefs.							
12	I use my clothes and accessories to express my culture.							
13	I'm aware of the best way to dress to support my career.							
14	Most of the clothes and accessories I own give me confidence and help me feel self-assured.							
15	The way I dress is important in giving me a sense of control over my life.							
16	I own clothes and accessories that remind me of happy moments in my life.							
17	I don't buy new clothes and accessories for every single occasion.							
18	I never rush to buy a new outfit. I wait to make sure I really like it and that it will have longevity.							
19	I don't own a broad selection of clothes that I've only worn once.							
20	I utilise cosmetics to express my creativity and showcase my inner beauty.							
21	I only buy clothes and accessories I feel a solid connection to.							
22	If I want to feel a certain way, I consider the clothes and accessories I'm wearing.							
23	I always treat my skincare routine as an opportunity for self-care.							
24	I explore a variety of hair and make-up styles to help me explore different parts of myself.							
25	I'm aware of the way different colours make me feel.							
26	I'm a walking mood ring. You can tell how I'm feeling by the clothes and accessories I'm wearing.							

27	I don't own a wide selection of clothes that no longer fit me.								
28	When I'm dissatisfied with a part of my physical appearance, I wear clothing that draws attention away from it.								
29	I wear clothes that showcase the parts of my physical appearance that satisfy me.								
30	I regularly shake up my personal style.								
31	I rarely get upset when I don't fit into a particular clothing size.								
32	I never claim to have nothing to wear.								
33	I rarely worry about being over- or underdressed when I go out.								
34	I don't confine myself to a signature style. Instead, my wardrobe allows me to easily explore a variety of styles.								
35	After I get dressed, I always check to make sure I feel comfortable.								
36	I often customise my clothes to make sure they're a good fit.								
	Totals								
	Grand total								

Quiz adapted from Samreen, N. (2014), 'Proximity of clothing to self-concept: Understanding differences across the demographics in Pakistan'. *European Journal of Business and Management*, 6 (18), 100–101.

'Clothing is not a random decision, but an unspoken yet important language which tells many things about us; our personality traits, attitudes, social position and our take on life.'

Nida Samreen

Results

Total: 169–252 – Big Dress Energy

A score within this range means you have Big Dress Energy: a solid and healthy relationship with your wardrobe and overall appearance. You regularly curate mindful looks that speak to your most authentic self, and as such, you turn your style into an act of self-love. You allow your clothes, accessories, hairstyles and cosmetic choices to celebrate your body while honouring your changing moods and attitudes towards it. It's also easy for you to let your clothes speak on your behalf because you know precisely what they're saying. When you wear an outfit with Big Dress Energy, you just know you're killing it.

With all of the pressures we face, from social media to our own insecurities, maintaining this energy is not always easy. It's simpler to just follow a trend and keep buying stuff in the hope that it will help you feel something. Consider the coming lessons as a road map to keep you on the right path. At the end of this journey, you'll be able to use psychology to understand what it is that you really want and how to appear as your best self so you can stop clogging your closet and feeding your most basic impulses with sale items.

Total: 85–168 – Medium Dress Energy

Most people find themselves somewhere within this range. Perhaps you know the basics of fashion psychology, but you don't know how to take your style to the next level. The 'dress' in Big Dress Energy doesn't refer to a literal dress by the way. I'm not expecting everyone to start going to the cinema in a poufy dress by British designer Molly Goddard (who somehow managed to make ten pounds of tulle look effortlessly cool). You could be wearing a basic pair of jeans and a plain white T-shirt and still exude Big Dress Energy. The 'next level' is about ensuring that your sense of style and the things you choose to buy serve the right purpose. That purpose has to be dictated by you. But how can you know what that purpose is if you don't take a beat and ask yourself the right questions? Each chapter of this book is purposely designed to challenge you and put you in a state of self-reflection so you can stop thoughtlessly dressing and evolve from Medium to Big Dress Energy.

Total: 1–84 – Small Dress Energy

Oh Hunny, if you're in this range, go ahead and read this book twice for me. We'll get through this together.

Come with me, we have work to do

I've worked with global brands like Next, Stitch Fix and Afterpay. I've had my thesis published in the *International Journal of Market Research*. I've been featured in almost every major publication, from *Forbes* to the *Wall Street Journal* to *Harper's Bazaar* and many more. I've achieved all of this because I just can't shut up about fashion psychology. You know that feeling when you watch a good documentary, and you have a burning desire to tell everyone and their grandmother about it? That's how I feel all the time. I will never be able to explain just how much it warms my heart to know that this once incredibly niche topic will be embraced by so many people.

This will be a fun but by no means content-light read, by the way.

Every page is jam-packed with useful information, and I'm hoping the studies featured will blow your mind (if only just a little bit) and resonate with you in unforgettable ways. So let me ease you in by offering a breakdown of what to expect: Chapters 1 to 6 are designed to alter the way you consider your personal style, and will delve deeply into the power of clothes to explain all the different ways in which your outfit choices impact how you navigate day-to-day life. This knowledge will serve as a foundation so that by the time you get to Chapters 7 and 8, where you'll be revamping your wardrobe and doing away with your old shopping habits, the process will be a lot less daunting. You'll be equipped with every insight needed to tackle these challenges head-on. Big Dress Energy doesn't just start from the neck down, though, so in Chapter 9 we'll move beyond clothes and accessories and uncover all there is to know about beauty psychology. This will be a deep dive into the holy trinity that some call the 'jewellery of the face': skincare, cosmetics and hair. At the end of each chapter, I'll provide key takeaways to help you fully digest all of the lessons we've learned. So, without further ado, let's get cracking.

Chapter 1

It's giving what it's supposed to

How to dress with your identity and external perceptions in mind

'Dress like there's no tomorrow. And then
tomorrow, do it again!'

Dorit Kemsley

If you follow the institution that is *The Real Housewives of Beverly Hills*, then you're well aware of Dorit Kemsley's commitment to her outfits. If you don't, then the best way I can explain it is by asking you to imagine someone doing a big shop in Tesco, but dressed as if they're accepting an award at the Grammys. If your reaction is to roll your eyes, then you'll join many of the show's fans and some of Dorit's co-stars, who malign the housewife for doing 'the most'. OK, true, some of her looks can be a bit out of place. Even as a self-confessed over-dresser, I too thought stilettos to a family barbecue was a bit much, but

I commend Dorit for her commitment to dressing in a way that feels authentic to her.

People will always judge others for being *too* interested in fashion. They'll tell you that being concerned with your personal style makes you vapid, materialistic and shallow. I've definitely been on the receiving end of that kind of criticism. Let's take a moment to ask those people one very rhetorical question, delivered with a squint and a slight tilt of the head: 'Should we all just dress like prisoners instead?' No, seriously, I often wonder how happy these people would be if the world transformed into the set of *Squid Game*, leaving us with only a green tracksuit, a pair of black plimsolls and an embroidered three-digit number to differentiate us. Sure, it would be a lot easier to get dressed in the morning in this fashion-free utopia, but, as I will explain in this chapter, those extra minutes you save won't be even the slightest bit worth it.

When we talk about fashion, the question should never be whether you care about it or not, because that's simply irrelevant. It's irrelevant because you are constantly communicating through your styling choices, whether intentionally or unintentionally. You're also constantly making assessments about other people based on their styling choices. You might be thinking, 'But I don't judge books by their cover!' Hush, my dear, we all do – and we do it because the way we dress or 'cover' ourselves is important. First impressions occur within the blink of an eye, so it's your outward appearance, including your clothes, that speak for you.

I know the thought of your clothes having such a considerable impact might feel worrying, but it really shouldn't. Fear not; my aim is for this book to inspire you to a higher level of self-awareness when it comes to your personal style. I want to empower you to really think about how the way you dress represents you beyond the surface level, and how it influences the way you're treated by those around you.

Who wore it best? Your style, according to your different selves

> 'We use clothing as this paradoxical combination of camouflage and self-revelation, a shield for and stripping to our basic humanity.'
>
> *Maria Popova, writer and founder of* The Marginalian

I've talked about how clothes have the power to help you embody your true self – your essential being. Psychologists have been exploring this concept for years, but a 2000 study by Alison Guy and Maura Banim provides arguably the best explanation. The pair investigated the relationship between clothing and the self over several weeks by getting a group of participants to engage in a range of tasks, such as keeping a clothing diary, completing a wardrobe interview and providing a detailed response to the question: 'What do clothes mean to me?' After gathering all that data, the psychologists concluded that we have a dynamic relationship with clothing that affects the different ways we view ourselves according to the following three categories:

1. The person you hope to be
2. The person you fear to be
3. The person you are most of the time

When we get dressed, we can appear as the person we hope to be if we wear clothes that 'formulate positive self-projections'.[1] That's psychologist speak for clothes that make you feel like the shit and give you confidence – basically, outfits that give Big Dress Energy. We're more prone to dress this way when we take the necessary steps to level up psychologically and emotionally and then decide to physically display this internal change. Wearing those favourite pieces helps to bridge the gap between you now and the ultimate version of you. For some, it could be a luxury accessory acting as a gateway to a more financially stable self; for others it might be a vintage jacket that signals the entry point to a more sustainable lifestyle.

The second and slightly scary category, the person you fear to be, speaks to all the times you wear things that, for whatever reason, just don't work. We slip into this category when our wardrobes become a physical manifestation of any negative thoughts and feelings we're experiencing. It's also the negative version of us that appears when we wear deeply unflattering clothes, or dress in a way that draws attention to the parts of us we like the least. For me, this came in the form of the scruffy jumpers and decade-old, holey leggings that I often wore on the school run. Sadly, my big sister passed away when my niece and nephew were just two and five years old. Suddenly, at the age of twenty-five, I went from going to after-work drinks to hanging out with grandmothers in the playground at 3.15pm. It just wasn't how I had envisioned my life going, and those trips were a constant reminder of my grief, from which, at times, I feared I would never heal. Without realising it, the utter lack of care I put into my outfits for these school runs served as the external projection of my internal fear (we'll look more closely at the role of clothing in challenging difficult emotions in Chapter 5).

While categories one and two represent the highs and lows of the role clothing plays in self-presentation, category three – the person you are most of the time – is the most consistent and stable. These are your go-to outfits. They're the clothes that signify who you are most of the time and arguably showcase your most authentic self.

While a lot of this might seem a bit daunting, Guy and Banim concluded that our relationship with our clothes is both 'ongoing and dynamic', and that our clothes act as a 'major source of enjoyment' because they help us navigate between these different versions of ourselves.

Equally, many people don't realise that the clothes we *don't* buy are also significant. The clothes that we put in our shopping basket and the clothes that make us wince and ask, 'Who would ever buy that?!' all form part of our likes and dislikes, and so combine to say something about who we are.

> 'Appearance is at least as important in establishment and maintenance of the self as verbal communication.'
>
> Gregory P. Stone, psychologist at Arizona State University

If you think of yourself as fearless and bold, but you make very conservative fashion choices, a discrepancy will exist between the reflection in the mirror and the true you. A psychologist named Edward Tory Higgins discovered this back in 1987 and called it 'Self-Discrepancy Theory'. According to this theory, a discrepancy between who you are and how you dress can result in a range of nasty side effects, including lower self-esteem and a lack of pride.

Cultivating a wardrobe that is closer to the person we hope to be is a choice most of us can make, yet we often fall into a habit of wearing the same old things and dressing like the person we *fear* to be. This might be due to a lack of confidence or simply being stuck in rut – only you can truly know. Even if you take the necessary actions to become the person you've always wanted to be, the profound relationship between clothing and *self* means that if your style doesn't evolve with you, the side effects that Higgins describes will probably remain.

Fashion psychology tip

If more than one of the outfits you've worn this week fall into the *person you fear to be* category, you need to take a step back and consider why that is. Start by asking yourself two questions:

- What do you need to do to get closer to the person you hope to be?
- What does the person you hope to be look like?

Outfits belonging to the person you fear to be probably mean very little to you. That's why it's so important to consider the true value of the clothes you're wearing. In doing so, you'll be able to process how you can better use your clothing choices as a tool to embody the best version of you. Allowing your clothes to work for you in this way will reduce any psychological discrepancy and positively benefit your mental well-being.

As the frontier between the self and the 'not self' (anything and everything that is inauthentic to who you are), style is first and foremost about seeking approval from the person who matters most – you. Then, it's about solidifying your place in the world, and this is where other people get involved. We've just talked about the role of style and the self, where 'self' refers to your sense of who you are and what you are. In the following pages, we will look at the role of style in identity. Identity is your 'social self': the meaning you apply to your 'self', negotiated via your everyday interactions with other people.[2]

Which identity are you verifying today?

When I think about the question 'Who are you?', my brain always conjures up images of fingers flicking quickly through countless files in a drawer marked 'Identity'. Often my answer is simply, 'a Black, cis-gendered woman', but the more I think about it, the more descriptors I add to that sentence – and before you know it, I'm left with a pretty long list.

On LinkedIn, I add 'fashion psychologist' to that list. During my school days, 'Catholic' made an appearance. When I spend time with my family, 'Trini' pops up, and when I speak to my American friends, 'Londoner' gets tacked on. On Instagram, I've been known to identify as a 'baddie'. On TikTok, a 'dancer'. On Hinge, 'single and looking for love' (although I'm hoping that will no longer be applicable by the time this book is out). As you can see, identity is fluid – our identities are subject to change, and on many occasions, they overlap. As a result, it's often difficult to express who you are in words, so your appearance and how you choose to style yourself helps you to articulate your identity in the messiness of everyday life.

Your clothes can visually express multiple overlapping identities, like your age, gender, race, culture, social class, sexuality, politics and personal interests. Even the saying 'wearing different hats' is a comment on how different outfits spotlight different facets of our identity. For example, I'm more Trini than Londoner when I'm draped in the sequins and feathers that constitute my carnival costume, and more fashion psychologist than Insta-baddie when I'm wearing my best power suit. However, I'm still all of these things – and more.

Clothes also assuage the common fear of a lack of control. They give us autonomy over our individuality,[3] and can act as a vehicle to showcase our emotions when we simply don't feel like talking. Who hasn't worn headphones (even when nothing is actually playing), a massive hoodie or other items of what I call the 'socially distanced outfit' to ward off the threat of conversation on a terrible day?

Clothes also give you the power to cultivate the identities you present to the world, allowing you to reveal and conceal as you please. One example is the popularity of the fake designer bag. For every 'It' bag, there will be a fake. It will continue to be this way until people stop making bags. In their Menswear Fall/Winter 2020 runway collection, even Gucci made fun of this phenomenon by embossing the wording 'FAKE' across the collection, citing 'a playful commentary on the idea of imitation'. On the surface, the popularity of fakes can simply be seen as the desire to own something you can't afford. On the other hand, it also illustrates how we can use clothes and accessories to conceal our true social class.

When I spoke to Joanne Entwistle, author of *The Fashioned Body* (which is essentially the holy grail of all things fashion and identity), she explained: 'We occupy multiple positions in the world; we have multiple roles that we play. Identity is always in process. We're always changing, we're always evolving, but identity is stabilised through clothing.'

Part of the gang

Another important thing that our clothes communicate is our inherent need to belong, which is fundamental to who we are as human beings. Even on our off-days, on our 'I hate people' days, at our core, we're social beings and our desire to belong is crucial to developing our social identity. Another theory for you to learn, social identity theory, was developed by psychologists Henri Tajfel and John Turner in 1979, and explains how our identities are wrapped up in the groups with which we affiliate. This includes everything from being a twenty-something to a diehard member of the Beyhive. Because our clothes are tools of communication, they can signal our group affiliation to like-minded people.[4]

So how do we dress in a way that speaks to our social identity? According to psychologists, there are two stages to this: programme and review. The programme stage refers to what happens every time you look in the mirror and assess whether your outfit is an accurate representation of your identity. Ask yourself, 'Is this look giving [insert chosen identity]?' If it's giving what it's supposed to, then you can happily leave the house and embrace the review stage. The review stage refers to others' reactions to your outfit. Your social identity is justified or validated when programme and review are aligned. When they're not, you may feel that the way you want to be perceived is being challenged.[5]

Think about the outfit you wore the last time you left the house. Why did you choose to wear it? On a scale of one to ten, where one is *a choice based solely on personal desires and wishes*, and ten is *a choice based entirely on what other people think*, what number would you give it? Most people give numbers at the lower end of the scale. They'll put a one or even a rebellious zero, because who cares what other people think about the way you're dressed, right? But often we unknowingly take style cues from the people we spend time with and seek to emulate their fashion choices, both as a means to reinforce our social identity and to feed our desire to belong. We tell ourselves that we're not influenced by others when we pick out an outfit, but frequently we'll end up adopting elements of our peers' style because this behaviour is rewarded. This pattern is seen most clearly in the workplace. One study found that a 'cohesive sense of style' in an office creates a better team spirit and even fosters higher productivity levels.

The research, funded by British retailer Debenhams also discovered that sixty-eight per cent of managers had a heightened awareness of staff with a similar style to them, who, in turn, 'gained brownie points'.[6] When people are asked to rate the qualities of others, they identify people who are dressed similarly to them as being better leaders. Still, no one wants to be a carbon copy of their colleagues. Throughout each chapter in this book, you'll learn how to consider the personal meaning behind every aspect of your appearance. Not only will this positively impact your mental well-being, but it will also give you the skills necessary to balance cohesion with individuality.

Often when people decide to put more effort into their style or to change up their look, they feel pressure to appear different. I've noticed people online moaning that they can't wear something because 'everyone has it' or 'it's played out'. Oh, please. Unless you are hand-making your own clothes on a remote island somewhere, you will always find similarities between your style and that of someone who shares a similar social identity. In the case of me and my best friend, the review stage is often hilarious. Several outings start with a game of 'bitch stole my look' that always ends in fits of laughter. Most recently, we met each other at the train station wearing exactly the same skirt, but in different colours. We'd even managed to style it similarly. Are these occurrences simply a result of the obligatory 'What are you wearing to this thing later?' phone call? Research by psychoanalyst Brenda Berger suggests otherwise. Her study found that considering the style of your fellow group members, even unconsciously, bolsters your confidence and creates a natural appeal.[7]

Inclusion, opposition, incompatibility, disdain or rejection can all be conjured through clothing.[8] Clothes have the power to open new doors, deepen our connections and solidify our place within society.[9] That's why it's essential to consider all of this when deciding what to wear.

Dressing inside the lines

I hope by now you feel emboldened with the knowledge that you have the power to strengthen or decentre a particular part of your selfhood or identity through the simple act of getting dressed. However, my duty as your (favourite) fashion psychologist is to give you some necessary but slightly harsh truths. As much as we like to think of ourselves as entirely autonomous beings with the freedom to dress precisely as we want to all the time, this is sadly not the case. As Joanne explained to me, 'We're always fitting or hitting norms.' There will always be a battle between your personal desires and society's expectations, and that's just one example of the many limitations we must navigate when deciding how to style ourselves. Here, I will highlight a few more and give you some tips on dealing with them.

Limitation: Your body

This is a personal one for me as I have battled with my body since the age of twelve, when I was diagnosed with Ehlers-Danlos syndrome. This rare connective tissue disorder makes me super-duper flexible (splits are my go-to party trick) and causes chronic pain in around ninety per cent of my body. That's the worst thing about it. The second worst thing is that it's invisible, so people have difficulty understanding how bad the pain can get. The third worst thing is that no one knows what the hell it is, so you have to do a lot of explaining. But the fourth worst thing is that it can stop me from dressing the way I really want. On bad ankle days, heels are out of the question. On bad everything days, certain fits and fabrics just won't do.

From chronic pain to body dysmorphia, our bodies can come with a lot of baggage, and it's certainly not an uncommon experience. A 2019 YouGov survey revealed that thirty-five per cent of adults felt depressed because of their body image, and thirty-one per cent of teenagers felt ashamed for the same reason.[10] Negative feelings about your body can limit you from experimenting with new styles or wearing clothes for the person you hope to be, because you're afraid of standing out from the crowd. For many, it's easy to see clothes as another challenge to overcome.

Solution

First and foremost, your clothes should ensure that you feel both physically and psychologically comfortable. You can't simply dress your way out of things like chronic pain or body-image issues, but your clothes do have the power to make things a little easier. Start by acknowledging the parts of your body you like and dress with those areas in mind. For example, I adore my waist but I'm less impressed with my thighs, so I gravitate towards styles that accentuate my waist. This enables me to shift my focus and think of my body overall in a more positive light.

Take a moment to think about the areas of your body that you like and how you can use your clothes to shine a brighter light on them. Even if it's just your wrists – layer those bracelets and give the people wrists for days!

Another tip is to always place comfort at the heart of whatever you choose to wear. Sure, this may mean you have to let go of the outfit you'd planned in your head, but it will help you in other, fundamental ways. Studies have found that being comfortable in your clothes positively influences your cognition – your ability to learn and understand things. In one study, psychologists compared students' test scores while wearing comfortable and uncomfortable clothing. The results found that students wearing comfortable clothing performed significantly better and had higher scores than those wearing uncomfortable clothes.[11] As much as I love my six-inchers, they're by no means my only option. Dressing comfortably doesn't mean you have to completely compromise on your style. It's all about shifting your mindset from predominantly thinking about how you look and more towards considering how you feel. When I think in this way, I feel less disheartened about having to adapt my outfit, because I know wearing something more comfortable is literally the smarter decision.

Limitation: Money

'Once I start making some serious money, it's over for you hoes.' That tweet stays in my bookmarks because of how incredibly relatable it is. Who among us hasn't dreamed of the significant style overhaul that you'd indulge in if you happened to win a couple mill in the lottery? Stunting on your evil old manager in dripped-down designer gear will, of course, be a top priority, but having more disposable income also gives you the power to be more intentional with the brands you buy. While you definitely won't need millions, it's a fact that brands that abide by ethical and sustainable practices and produce clothes that are built to last are generally more expensive than what we think of as fast-fashion labels. When your pockets are a bit on the lighter side, it gets harder to resist the siren song of cheap, trend-led fashions. Luckily, there are three solutions to help you fight back.

Solutions

1. RENT YOUR WARDROBE.

Clothing rental platforms like By Rotation, Hurr and Girl Meets Dress are continuing to gain popularity. Even luxury brands and retailers like Selfridges and Burberry are jumping on the rental wave, making it easier than ever to dress like the person you hope to be without going into debt.

2. SHOP SECOND-HAND

Finding a lightly used genuine Louis Vuitton scarf in a charity shop for £120 (down from £600) used to sound like an urban myth, but the second-hand retail market is booming and finds like these are now incredibly common. And with sites like Vestiaire Collective and good old eBay, you don't even have to go hunting in person to find iconic pre-owned pieces. Just make sure you're spending wisely and considering quality, not quantity. (For more on budgeting and mindful shopping, see Chapter 8.)

3. STEP YOUR MONEY UP

Pretty self-explanatory: find a way to boost your income.

Limitation: Age

Repeatedly, I've recommended an outfit to my mum and received a cutting one-word response: 'Mutton.' The concept of 'mutton dressed as lamb' is the mistaken belief that you can't wear something because it's too 'young' for you, and it's a belief that affects women in particular. When I worked with a client to investigate this concept, their survey results were shocking. Apparently, twenty-three is the age at which women are most commonly told to stop wearing something because they're 'too old', with the majority (sixty-five per cent) of these comments coming from family members and partners. Even from a young age, appearance has always had significant social consequences for women, who in turn feel social pressures to dress their age and dress in a way that conforms to societal (cough, sexist) standards.

Let's get a little more depressing before we jump to the solution part.

Limitation: Prejudice

Women don't only face pressure to dress differently due to ageism. We routinely second-guess our outfit choices depending on whether we have enough energy to battle the sexualisation of our bodies on a given day. In 1998, actress Rose McGowan wore a see-through chainmail dress to the red carpet of the VMA awards that sent shockwaves through the media. Now, when women dress in ways that showcase their bodies, they're often labelled as attention-seeking, amoral 'females' who are 'asking for it'. How many times have we heard of a woman's outfit being brought up in cases of someone else's sexual misconduct? A flash of cleavage and suddenly ridiculous and harmful ideas are apparently 'justified'. When this happens, the initial meaning or motivation behind the outfit is lost.

Twenty-one years after her red-carpet appearance, Rose revealed she actually wore the dress in response to a sexual assault. It was 'a political statement', a way to reclaim power over her body.[12] Not that the media ever cared.

Similarly, violence against transgender and gender non-conforming people is on the rise around the world. While society's expectations of gender roles are slowly changing, many people still feel pressured to wear clothing that conforms to an anachronistic binary at the cost of betraying their true selves. As Joanne reveals: 'There is nothing inherently masculine or feminine about specific items of clothing or clothing colours. Instead, gendered categorisations of clothing stem from norms and values that are prevalent in popular culture, for example, advertising that we're encouraged (and sometimes forced – by powerful conventions and prohibitions) to adhere to.'

Every day, people face discrimination, abuse and even violence due to prejudicial beliefs targeting their identity and, by extension, their clothing. In 2011, the French government made it illegal to wear a face-covering veil such as a niqab in public, and in 2021 the French Senate passed a bill that proposed to ban women under eighteen from wearing a hijab in public. Many Muslim women felt these laws violated their religious beliefs. Hiba Latreche, a twenty-two-year-old law student from Strasbourg, expressed her hurt to the *Guardian*: 'As a Muslim woman wearing a headscarf, I already experience Islamophobia in the public arena – instead of our legislators protecting us, they are actually making it legal.'[13]

In 2013, the Million Hoodie March was organised in New York City in response to the murder of Trayvon Martin, a seventeen-year-old Black boy whose name has now become synonymous with the Black Lives Matter movement. I investigated this tragic story for my undergraduate thesis, and while conducting my research, I couldn't shake a comment from American talk-show host Geraldo Rivera: 'I think the hoodie is as much responsible for Trayvon Martin's death as George Zimmerman was.' This comment illuminates the many ways in which clothing styles are consistently used as a weapon against Black and ethnic minority people. When a hoodie is draped over a Zuckerberg type, it's seen as edgy and innovative, but on a Black body, it's a reason to clutch your purse and cross the street. According to the Geraldo Riveras of the world, banning hoodies for young Black boys is enough to stop racism. Because that makes sense.

Solution(ish)

Earlier, I outlined the review stage of getting dressed and the role that other people's perceptions play in what we choose to wear. However, it's vital to identify those perceptions that are rooted in prejudice and discrimination. Figuring this out can be difficult because these types of prejudices are systemic, making it easy to internalise limiting beliefs about how we should and shouldn't be dressing – but that's still no reason to give up hope. As with most things you'll find in this book, the solution is rooted in asking yourself a few questions. When you feel yourself shying away from an outfit you really like, one that you feel best represents you, ask yourself if you would wear it if you were somebody else. If the answer is yes, then think about why someone else should have the right to explore this style if you don't?

Your age, race, religion and gender shouldn't stop you from expressing your identity through your clothes, but changing long-standing and antiquated beliefs doesn't happen overnight – especially when the law is not on your side. It starts with everyday people like you and me using our voices to challenge, be allies, pass the mic and empower those who need our support. The Hands off my Hijab! protest[14] and Million Hoodie March are just two examples of the power of everyday people coming together, showing compassion and demanding the freedom to be – and therefore dress – however the hell they want.

But it's also important to ask whether you're shying away from a style due to a legitimate limitation like cultural appropriation. There are lots of creative ways to bring different influences into your wardrobe – you don't have to be French to wear Breton stripes – but it's important not to adopt a style that the culture in question might find inappropriate, especially when unacknowledged. Research shows that when you carelessly adopt culturally rich styles with no acknowledgement of their origins, it can cause significant harm. Those whose culture has been appropriated can be left with a lower sense of self-esteem and a diminished sense of community worth.[15] On a personal level, if you choose to go down this route it's likely that your review stage will be full of (justified) hostility. It's just not worth it. In Chapter 5, I'll detail all of the great benefits you can achieve by leaning into styles reminiscent of your own culture to help you fully embrace more aspects of your identity.

> 'Just be confident about being who you are and dressing for that person.'
>
> *Tim Gunn*

Getting dressed seems simple enough. You put your trousers on one leg at a time, and the next thing you know, you've managed to conjure up an entire look. But it's not as simple as that. Getting dressed is an act of balancing competing factors, like social context, external perceptions and your identity, as well as your desire to both stand out and fit in.

Psychologists call it 'symbolic interactionism', which essentially means that the wearer of an outfit is 'active in determining the meaning of an item along with the viewer of that item'.[16]

Style guides can often make dressing seem black and white, fashionable versus unfashionable, but as you've just read, it's a lot more complicated than that. In the next chapter, I'll give you the cheat code. I'll reveal research that explains what different styles communicate and how you can use that knowledge to your advantage to make this balancing act a lot easier.

Key takeaways

★ It's important to wear clothes that are in alignment with how you view yourself to avoid experiencing the negative side effects of self-discrepancy, such as low self-esteem.

★ Avoid dressing like the person you fear to be by getting rid of clothes that are a physical manifestation of negative thoughts and feelings.

★ Identify the outfits that represent the best version of yourself or the person you hope to be and wear them more frequently.

★ Your clothes often signify your group affiliations, but you can obtain a sense of individuality by making a conscious effort to express the multifaceted nature of your identity through your outfits.

★ Body issues, social constructs, prejudices and financial burdens limit the extent to which we can use clothes as a tool of self-expression. Fight these limitations where you can. Where you can't, focus on making clothing choices that prioritise your physical and psychological comfort.

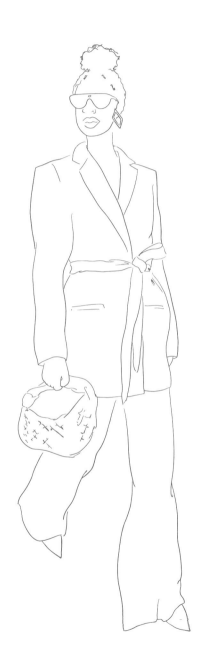

Chapter 2

Shh! Let the clothes do the talking

How to make sure your clothes are saying the right things

When we first meet someone, we know pretty quickly whether they'll be someone we want to get to know better, someone we won't give a second thought to or someone who'll become the main character in a hilarious group-chat anecdote. But how long do you think it actually takes to form a first impression?

Five minutes?

One minute?

Thirty seconds?

*Insert the loud 'incorrect' sound from *Family Fortunes*.*

Try *0.10 seconds*.[1] Yes, a study by psychologist Alex Todorov found that first impressions occur within one-tenth of a second! That's not even enough time to open your mouth, let alone share the devastatingly witty joke you've been keeping in your back pocket. So, what happens? Your outward appearance, including your clothes, speaks for you. People stress the importance of first impressions for a good reason – they're incredibly difficult to change. A little thing called 'confirmation bias' makes it harder for us to be given a second chance. Psychology shows that we unconsciously seek out opportunities to support or confirm our first impression of someone after we meet them. You thought that guy you just spoke to was an asshole? Now everything he does next, from how he walks to how he breathes, is likely to give off asshole energy. Making a good first impression may seem as easy as simply not being an asshole, but as I mentioned earlier, everyone (yes, including you) makes snap judgements based on first looks alone.

Studies show that your clothes can influence how much power people think you have, how much help they are willing to give you (yikes),[2] and the assumptions they make about your personality.[3] For a study investigating first impressions, psychologists based in the US asked a group of participants to send in pictures of the shoes they wore most.[4] These were then shown to a separate group, who were asked to make anonymous judgements about the unknown shoe-owners. These weren't just wishy-washy things like, 'What do you think this person is like?' They were asked to make concrete assumptions about the shoe owner's age, gender and income. Surprisingly, the results revealed that their assumptions were shockingly accurate. Remember, they saw nothing but pictures of these people's shoes, yet they were even able to correctly guess the shoe-owner's attachment style. The researchers concluded that this may be because: 'Anxious people crave attention and caring, which they might pursue through expressive decoration, selecting shoes designed to make them literally stand out. In contrast, individuals with avoidant attachment, who are more aloof and do not care how they are perceived, might engage in more indiscriminate shoe selection.'[5]

We often find ourselves wearing things that represent the 'person we are most of the time', and as this study reveals, other people are pretty good at analysing who that is. However, we're all constantly growing and evolving, so when our style doesn't evolve with us, the impression that we project won't match up with who we really are – and there are few things more frustrating than being misunderstood. Before you rush off to get a peek at your colleagues' loafers to try and guess what they're really like – and whether they're making more than you – don't forget to put your bookmark here.

Contrary to popular belief, 'main character syndrome' was not created by Gen Z on TikTok. In 1959, sociologist Erving Goffman suggested that we use our clothes to manage external perceptions because we see ourselves as actors and the world as our stage, borrowing the much older term 'dramaturgy'. In the same way that actors rely on costume designers to help the audience make accurate assumptions about their characters, everyday people like you and me use clothes as props to present ourselves to others in very specific ways. Our version of a standing ovation is when people look at us and think precisely what we hoped they would – a successful programme and review.

In her book *Fashion: The Key Concepts*, author Jennifer Craik does an impressive job of explaining the many ways in which clothes mirror language: 'We can think of fashion as a language made up of vocabulary (a collection of items of clothing typical of a culture), syntax (the rules about how clothes can be combined) and grammar (the system of arranging and relating garments and conventions of decoding and interpreting the meaning of a particular look).'[6]

This chapter will be your translator. My goal here is to help you discover the language of your personal style and reveal how people generally respond to different looks. But, of course, language is not universal. The research outlined throughout this chapter, and this book, was largely conducted on Western audiences, so the perceptions they generate are mostly indicative of people from a similar background. Despite these limitations, I've tried to explain the findings in a way that will feel universal and allow all readers to gain a better understanding of how their clothing style impacts the way in which they're perceived. That way, no matter where you are in the world, every time you get dressed, you'll be comforted with the knowledge that whatever your outfit is saying about you, it's intentional.

Dress for success

> 'Good clothes can't put an unqualified person in the boardroom, but bad clothes can keep a qualified person out.'
>
> *John T. Molloy, author of* Dress for Success[7]

Arguably one of the most complex parts of being an adult is attempting to cultivate a rewarding and lucrative career. Countless obstacles can interfere with your ascent up the career ladder, but there's one that's familiar to almost all of us. Coined in 1978 by psychologists Pauline Clance and Suzanne Imes, 'imposter syndrome' is the misguided belief that everyone else is somehow brighter, better and worthier than you. Up to eighty per cent of us have suffered from imposter syndrome at some point during our working lives, contributing to feelings of self-doubt and anxiety.[8] Unsurprisingly, women, and particularly women of colour, are the most likely to experience imposter syndrome. I can admit that when I was first approached to write this book, I initially put it down to luck. I had to actively fight against that thought process (and I still do at times) because imposter syndrome is such a pervasive experience. It affects big things, like your psychological state, as well as more minor things, like how you dress. Studies have shown that women are susceptible to different moods and these, particularly the negative ones, such as feelings of self-consciousness, influence our clothing choices to a greater extent than those who don't identify as women.[9] These feelings in turn, cause us to dress like the person we fear to be, which often means we select drab outfits that reflect our negative headspace.

It takes a lot of internal work to dig yourself out of such a low place and come to terms with the fact that you're deserving of your achievements. That work comes in many forms. For me, positive affirmations and social media breaks help a lot, but one thing we can all agree on is that it takes a lot of time. You can start by making some simple changes to your wardrobe to project an air of success, even when you're not really feeling it. This tactic has been proven to produce some real-world benefits.

Power-dressing

People have been using clothes to signify status ever since we progressed beyond the humble fig leaf, but the concept of 'power-dressing' didn't really take off until the 1980s, when women first made cracks in the glass ceiling of the corporate world. Loads of us look back at the extreme shoulder pads of that era and laugh, but studies show that those little pads played a big role in supporting women in male-dominated arenas. A 1997 study found that broad shoulders are typically associated with masculinity and that they positively correlate with the amount of testosterone you appear to have.[10] Shoulder pads became the go-to style for many women in the corporate arena, as they create the perception of broader shoulders and the illusion of a more masculine figure. A beautifully constructed blazer with a strong shoulder is still a solid look, but as time progresses and the old boys' clubs dwindle, it's no longer necessary to 'man-up' your wardrobe to achieve success. However, formal wear, including multiple suit variations, will always be at the top of the power-dressing pyramid for everyone.

Suit up

In his 1975 book *Dress for Success*, author John T. Molloy states that his extensive research on over 15,000 executives enabled him to develop the definitive guide to dressing your way to the top. Some of his recommendations haven't held up as well as others. I'm still unclear what he meant by 'a chalk stripe can label you as a Wall Street executive or a Chicago gangster'. Still, the importance he placed on formal wear being 'the garment on which most people judge the wearer's status, character and ability' still rings true.[11]

Whether it's a pantsuit, a skirt suit, a sharp dress or some quality shirts, if you don't possess a decent range of formal wear, then this is your reminder for your next shopping trip. So-called tech bros will have you thinking that formal wear is dead, but they all reach for their expensive suits when it's time to really get down to business. Formal wear is the ultimate symbol of authority. These clothes can often be the difference between people believing that you know what you're talking about or not. Researchers tested out this concept on therapists, asking them to conduct counselling sessions wearing either a smart dress, a shirt and tie, or blue jeans and a T-shirt. The analysis revealed that when therapists were dressed more formally, their clients reported a more significant reduction in their levels of distress than when their therapists were dressed casually.[12] Every time you step into a suit, you're increasing your social currency, positioning yourself as a more dominant presence and someone to be listened to.

Fashion psychology tip

Research suggests that you should always wear a high-quality suit when you're negotiating, whether it's business or personal. You're more likely to win a negotiation when wearing a suit because the person you're debating with perceives you as a more authoritative figure and 'decreases their own perception of social power'.[13]

Good tailoring goes a long way

As with everything you wear, you have to be thoughtful. Throwing on a dusty old suit in an attempt to be perceived as powerful will not achieve the desired results. For example, in an online study conducted by Hertfordshire-based psychologists to test how different suits impacted first impressions, over 200 people were shown two pictures. In the first, a faceless man wore a bespoke suit, and in the second, he wore a regular, off-the-rack suit. Participants were then asked to judge his character. After being exposed to each picture for just five seconds, the results revealed that wearing a bespoke suit can drastically change the way people think about you, encouraging them to view you as more confident, more successful, more flexible and better paid.[14] As people who wear bespoke suits are typically high earners, it can be argued that the halo effect came into play. The halo effect is the assumption that one good thing about a person suggests that they have a lot of other positive attributes too. In this case, the finer details of the bespoke suit communicated wealth and its common place for people to associate wealth with positive traits despite a lack of evidence to support that assumption.

Bespoke suits can be too pricey for many people, especially if your life-style doesn't require you to regularly dress formally. My takeaway from this research is that clothing fit is just as important as clothing style when it comes to first impressions. When I buy something new, I always go up a size, especially if it's a pair of trousers. I then make a quick trip to my local dry cleaner (hi Jim!) for some alterations, like reducing the waist or shortening the hem. When I'm feeling creative, I pick up my needle and thread, pop on a YouTube tutorial and have a go at the alterations myself. Before I know it, my outfit has gone from off-the-rack to made-to-measure. Clothes that enable you to easily make your own custom adjustments, such as wrap dresses, are also a great option. It's all about donning clothes that look like they were made for you and complement every aspect of your body. There's nothing worse than having to con-stantly tug at clothes that are either too loose or too tight when your goal is to evoke an air of authority. Not only do well-fitting clothes make you feel more comfortable, as the research shows, they also help you to rise in others' estimation.

Fashion psychology tip

Unless it's boiling out, try to layer it up. Studies have revealed that people who wear layers are perceived to be more competent than those wearing fewer layers or no layers at all.[15] Further studies have also found that layered looks present a more authoritative image for both men and women.[16]

Power clothes meet power pose

Next to appearance, body language is one of the most widely recognised forms of non-verbal communication. If you've gone to the trouble of using fashion psychology to pick a powerful outfit, don't ruin it by hunching your shoulders, hanging your head down and adopting other non-verbal cues that signal powerlessness. Even in the wider animal kingdom, such closed postures, which effectively shrink the body, have been linked to a lower status.[17] Want to avoid being at the bottom of the food chain? It's time to power-pose. First suggested by Dana Carney, Amy Cuddy and Andy Yap in their 2010 research paper, power poses don't just exhibit power – they *produce* it.[18] Power poses have been linked to extroversion, increased pain tolerance, a reduction of the stress-inducing hormone cortisol, and an increase in testosterone, which has been thought to increase dominance and competitiveness in men and women.[19]

Elevate the power of your power outfit by holding at least one of the following five poses for a couple of minutes. All you'll need is a quiet room with a chair and desk or table to get started.

- **Pose 1**: Stand up straight with your hands on your hips and your feet shoulder-width apart.
- **Pose 2**: Place the chair behind the desk or table, then sit down with your hands behind your head. Next, place your feet up on the desk or table.
- **Pose 3**: Stand up straight, lean over and place your hands on the desk or table with your fingers spread out.
- **Pose 4**: Stand up straight with your feet hip-distance apart and hold your hands wide above your head.
- **Pose 5**: Sit on the chair with your legs spread wide apart. Place one hand on your lap and drape the other over whatever piece of furniture is adjacent to you.

OK, suit up – but don't be boring

Embodying Big Dress Energy means doing away with formulaic dressing. Wearing a suit to showcase authority might seem pretty obvious, but you shouldn't just rush to pick the first boring grey suit you find. You need to add some spice to your outfits if you want to really make an impact and assert your authority. In a 2021 study titled 'Clothes Make the Leader', psychologists discovered that dressing outside the box can lead to an increase in approval and charisma ratings in the world of work. In the previous chapter, I revealed how people are drawn to those who dress similarly to them and how this can happen unconsciously. However, you should always endeavour to inject elements of your own personality and unique tastes into your power-dressing wardrobe. Similar studies have also shown that while conservative styles can give the appearance of someone who is 'self-controlled, understanding and reliable', more daring clothing styles give the impression that you're 'more attractive and individualistic'.[20]

Personally, brightly coloured suits are a bit of me. Right now, I own a yellow suit, a purple one, a pink one and a sky-blue blazer, all tailored to within an inch of their life. You don't have to be as bold as me (or Steve Harvey), though. Instead, you can lean on the power of your accessories. A quirky sock here and a statement watch there can go a long way towards cementing your status as someone of whom others should take note. Funnily enough, it can even put some money in your pocket. In a study on tipping behaviour, researchers found that diners left larger tips for waitresses who wore flowers in their hair than they did when the same waitresses served them without the flowers.[21] Psychologists suggest that wearing such striking accessories makes you appear more appealing and attracts wealth. Getting random strangers to comply with you can be as easy as making a quick trip to Claire's Accessories.

All that glitters is good

'I like for jewellery to tell a story and to be able to talk about what I'm wearing. That's more important to me than a name, brand or label.'

Nikki Reed

If people thought about their clothes in the same way they thought about their jewellery, there would be little reason for this book to exist. Both can be mass-produced, but somehow jewellery is perceived as having inherent value. I know I'm right in assuming that all of those watches, necklaces, earrings and rings that you lovingly store in pretty display boxes feel incredibly unique to you. Jewellery is multifaceted. It can be what psychologists call a 'transitional object' that acts as a source of comfort, soothing you and transporting you to happier times. It can be a 'status object', signalling everything from your wealth, social status, religious beliefs, and romantic availability. When I referenced the 'items' that make up the elements of a 'socially distanced outfit' in the previous chapter, jewellery was not one of them. I can't count the number of times a piece of jewellery has sparked a conversation with a complete stranger. Jewellery is great for first impressions because it acts as a window into your soul and as an invitation for people to get to know more about you. I would even go as far as saying that all jewellery is statement jewellery.

Why is jewellery capable of making such an impact? To answer this, evolutionary psychologists want you to go back – way back, back into time (word to Jimmy Castor). They argue that our attraction to shiny or sparkly objects stems from our innate need to seek water as a valuable resource. Objects with reflective surfaces remind us of that and are therefore alluring. It's certainly true that our affinity for jewellery dates back to when hunting and gathering involved more than ordering from Deliveroo. Shell beads unearthed by archaeologists in Morocco have confirmed that humans have been 'wearing and trading symbolic jewellery as early as 80,000 years ago'.[22] Just like my ancestors, I have a particular obsession with jewellery that began before I was capable of forming a proper sentence. In Caribbean culture, it's customary to pierce a little girl's ears when she's very young. I was rocking a pair of gold studs at just six months old, and I've seldom left home without a pair of earrings since. To date, my top five pieces, in no particular order, would have to be:

- the gold hoops from Trinidad that I 'borrowed' from my mum
- a single silver faux diamond pendant necklace that I 'borrowed' from my best friend Alysha (I promise I do buy my own stuff)
- a necklace from ASOS that has the Bobby McFerrin song lyrics 'Don't worry, be happy', which I bought with my pocket money at the age of fifteen (many a conversation has been sparked by that necklace)
- an earring and necklace set with the outline of Africa from Black-owned British brand Omolola jewellery, which I purchased along with my other best friend, Holly
- a massive pair of earrings in the shape of a Black woman created by Black artist Dorcas Magbadelo, which I got as a thank you for my contribution to the book *Grown: A Black girl's guide to growing up*.

When you put so much thought into the pieces of jewellery you own (or 'borrow'), they serve as a solid form of non-verbal communication. These pieces don't necessarily communicate anything about my status, which may be what you're looking for when you're dressing for success. However, what they're successful at doing is sharing a bit about my culture, my music tastes, my achievements, my personality and the things I value. People who appreciate what your jewellery communicates will naturally gravitate towards you.

In the 1967 book *How to Dress for Success* – clearly a trendy subject back in the day – author and celebrity costume designer Edith Head states that going overboard with your 'Successories' can be a recipe for disaster. She states that: 'Accessories might well be thought of as the "seasoning of your costume" and as every good cook knows, while seasoning is the secret of culinary success, too much salt or an overdose of pepper can ruin the sauce.' Not to disagree with a legend, but I believe that jewellery is too powerful to limit yourself in such a way. I don't subscribe to the Coco Chanel 'take one item off before you leave the house' school of thought, either. Sometimes, more is more.

Walk this way

'Shoes transform your body language and attitude. They lift you physically and emotionally.'

Christian Louboutin

The benefits of shoes certainly extend beyond their functional purpose. As the literal intersection between your body and the surrounding physical space, every step you take is drenched in meaning. As mentioned earlier, so much information can be garnered by a quick glance at your favourite pair of shoes, which is what makes them a crucial element of any good first-impression outfit. But which specific pair will help you to dress for success? You guessed it – heels.

I don't think I know of a more universal example of a love–hate relationship. You won't have to surf the internet for very long to learn all about the dangers that come with prancing about in heels. All my heel-loving associates have a story about an evening cut short by shoes, either by a twisted ankle or a sole that burned so badly, it felt like it had caught fire. Who among us didn't celebrate actress Nicola Thorp in 2017 when she petitioned the British government to stop women from being forced to wear high heels at work, after she'd refused to and was subsequently sent home from her job as a receptionist in the financial district?[23] And yet, we still covet them. Those tiny stilts have a grip on us because our physical pain is often dulled by the psychological comfort they bring.

There's no denying the feeling of sheer strength that comes from stepping into a pair of heels. Heels create a sense of power, simply by making us appear taller. A study analysing US presidential elections discovered that taller candidates are always more likely to win because we generally tend to associate height with authority.[24] Donald Trump's six feet two inches to Joe Biden's five feet ten inches is the exception to the rule here. Still, I suspect that you lose a bit of that height-related authority when you purposefully dismantle the fabric of democracy and act like a toddler having a tantrum.

Our association between height and authority is so pervasive that powerful people tend to overestimate their own height.[25] And no one is more influenced by the effects of height than men. One study discovered that even when their feet are not visible, men perceive women as being more sophisticated when wearing heels, suggesting a link between height and perceived elegance.[26] A similar study conducted in France observed that men are more willing to help a woman in heels than a woman wearing flats.[27] Who would have figured that the damsel in distress trope came with a specific dress code?

Now, there's no need to risk face-planting the floor in six-inch stilettos if that's not what you're used to. After all, anything that makes you uncomfortable is sure to knock your confidence and reduce any perceived power you may have gained. 'No pain, no gain' is an outmoded way of thinking. These days, we've been blessed with options. From platforms to flatform trainers and even heeled Crocs, the heels now exist that can project an air of power while maintaining your comfort. Like Cinderella, you simply have to find the perfect pair for you – just try not to lose them.

Label mates

'Luxury bags make your life more pleasant, make
you dream big, give you confidence and show your
neighbours you're doing well.'

Karl Lagerfeld

When it comes to power-dressing, respect is spelt with a L.A.U.R.E.N.T. To clarify, I want you to imagine a scenario where you're out running your daily errands, and you encounter a queue. If you're British like me, it shouldn't be too hard. Do you know how many times I've been gently scolded for jumping a queue that I didn't even know existed? Lord, do we love an organised queue! Anyway, back to the scenario: so you're in this imaginary queue, slowly edging towards the front, when suddenly a person carrying a sickening Saint Laurent bag from the new season collection cuts in front of you. What do you do?

Now, imagine a second scenario: you're in the same position, but the person that cuts in front of you is carrying a plain tote bag. I'm sure you're probably thinking, 'What the hell does the person's bag have to do with how I would react to their inconsiderate behaviour?' Please, let me land and don't shoot the messenger. Research suggests that people are more docile when confronted with luxury items. In one particular study, researchers driving either an expensive luxury car or a more affordable economy car stopped at a green light. Eighty-four per cent of the drivers behind the economy car immediately began sounding their horns in annoyance, with some going so far as to rear-end the poor researcher. However, when drivers found themselves stationed behind the luxury car, patience was suddenly a virtue. In this case, fifty per cent of drivers waited behind the luxury car in silence until it drove off, failing to sound their horn even once.[28]

I've never been a label whore, but I'm not blind to the positive associations that come with a designer tag. Time and time again, research has highlighted the social benefits of being attached to recognisable luxury brands. In a 2011 study investigating compliance, researchers got participants to walk around with a clipboard and approach unaccompanied shoppers to try and get them to stop and answer a few questions. The participants who approached the shoppers wore either a Tommy Hilfiger jumper or a plain, unbranded one. If you're a person who lowers their gaze, quickens their steps and even crosses the street at the mere sight of a stranger with a clipboard, you're probably thinking, 'Nothing short of a meteor strike could get me to stop.' Again, results suggest otherwise. The researchers found that when a participant wore the plain jumper, shoppers stopped and complied 13.6 per cent of the time. On the other hand, when they wore the Tommy Hilfiger jumper, the number of shoppers who answered the participant's questions jumped up to 52.2 per cent.[29]

Bringing out the name brands doesn't just improve your chances of receiving better treatment, it can also have a specific impact on the impression you give others. A study conducted in 2020 by psychologists from New York University and Princeton University revealed how economic status cues impact perceptions. They showed participants a series of random pictures of people's faces in a classic Zoom-video style, from the chest up. The people in the pictures were either wearing a luxury top or a cheaper, unbranded one. Even though participants were explicitly instructed to ignore everything except the faces in the pictures, over eighty-three per cent of the faces were perceived as being 'more competent' when they were wearing the luxury top.

What makes something 'luxury' is that it's highly coveted, of excellent quality and hard to come by. As I will explain in Chapter 4, people often embody the traits they associate with their clothes. So it's also possible that people have a more favourable first impression of those wearing luxury because they seem to embody a sense of luxury and project an air of superiority. It's also what my old psychology professor Adrian Furnham calls 'possession-defined success'[30] – *I wear luxury, therefore I am luxurious.*

If you already own luxury pieces, the science suggests that they'll be a fantastic addition to any power-dressing outfit. If you don't, here are two things you don't want to do:

Don't buy a fake

You may think that no one will notice whether the label on your fake Gucci bag is slightly misshapen or if the colour gradients are not quite right, but they may notice a change in your behaviour. Research carried out by Francesca Gino from the University of North Carolina found that wearing counterfeit products makes people behave more dishonestly. After her findings showed that people's moral choices are affected when they wear fake designer goods, Gino concluded: 'Feeling like a fraud makes people more likely to commit fraud.'[31] I don't know about you, but feeling the hefty hand of a security guard on your shoulder saying 'come with me' is not my cup of tea.

Don't buy something you can't afford

As I've grown over the years, I've become more sensible with my money and have come to accept that owning a designer bag containing a maxed-out credit card is not the way to go. Anything worth having is worth saving for – and, until you get there, feel free to rent away. That way, when you pull the trigger on your ultimate 'It' bag or your first designer piece, you'll be able to make an informed decision based on your lived experience.

Fashion psychology tip

Trends are often demonised for their lack of longevity, but research has identified that people who wear in-fashion clothing are perceived as more sociable. This doesn't mean you should constantly buy the current season's 'It' items. Instead, you can look at what you already own that resembles trending pieces and incorporate those items into your everyday style. The good thing about fashion being cyclical is that it gets harder to be caught off guard by 'new' trends when you reach a certain age. The Dior saddlebag, first released by John Galliano in 1999, shooting back into the spotlight in 2018 is a perfect example of this.

The Goldilocks principle

If an outfit that consists of a suit, high heels and a designer bag scares you, fear not. There's more to dressing for success than that. I'm guessing if you look back on all the people you've met that have given off a great impression, they didn't all dress the same. Dressing for success is not exclusively about wearing clothes that evoke a sense of power. It's also about dressing in a way that makes you come across as a warm, endearing person that people want to get to know better. To some, power and warmth may seem like competing ideas, but balancing these positive traits in your outfit is as easy as evoking the Goldilocks principle.

The Goldilocks principle is essentially the idea that taking a little bit of this and a little bit of that is where it's at. Putting her criminal trespassing aside, Goldilocks correctly identified that psychological well-being is often found not in the extremes, but when there is a sufficient balance between the simple and elaborate ends of the spectrum. What's more, equally satisfying your need to stand out with your need to fit in does wonders for your sense of self.[32]

Research shows that while people certainly feel more authoritative and competent when wearing formal attire, they are at their friendliest when wearing casual clothing. A study on teachers discovered that those dressed more casually in jeans were seen as being more sociable, outgoing and interesting.[33] Whether you call it high-low dressing or casual-chic, there is a beauty in achieving balance. So go ahead and pair your 'It' bag with a colourful loungewear set; wear a hoodie under a blazer or pair a serious shirt with some laid-back denim. My goal for you is to take bits and pieces from the research I've outlined in this chapter and construct an outfit that helps you to dress according to your version of success: one that Goldy would say is 'jussst right'.

Fashion psychology tip

If you're opting to wear jeans but still want to project a sense of authority, then reach for darker denim. Research shows that dark-coloured jeans are associated with higher prices, and as such, the wearer is seen as having more access to resources and, therefore, as being more powerful.[34]

Key takeaways

★ First impressions occur within 0.10 seconds. In that time, your clothes do all the talking for you, so it's important to be intentional when dressing.

★ Power-dressing and power-posing are simple yet effective tools to tackle issues like imposter syndrome.

★ Tailored clothes and formal wear increase your social currency and make you appear more authoritative. Meanwhile, opting for something casual will make you appear more friendly. You can adopt the Goldilocks principle by embracing high-low (formal + casual) dressing to get the best of both worlds.

★ People act more submissively when faced with luxury items due to the assumption that the wearer has better resources and wields more power.

★ Incorporate expressive accessories and jewellery into your outfits to give people a deeper insight into who you are, and to help you appear more individualistic.

Chapter 3

Embrace the rainbow

How to harness the power of colour psychology

'Colours, like features, follow the changes of the emotions.'

Pablo Picasso

I'll never forget being knee-deep into my fashion psychology degree when one of my classmates enthusiastically asked our lecturer if, at some point, we would learn about colour psychology. 'No. That's not really a thing,' was the curt reply, and we swiftly moved on to learn about statistics or ethics or whatever; my memory gets hazy after that. I just remember glancing over at my classmate's deflated face and feeling a weird mixture of sympathy and relief. You know that feeling when someone does something *you* were planning to do, and you get to witness the consequences play out in front of you? Colour psychology has always been treated with an air of scepticism by everyone who has ever taught me. While that never sat right with me, I kind of get it. There is a lot of bogus information out there that has overshadowed the very valid research conducted by scientists and theorists over the last few centuries.

'Getting your colours done' used to be super popular back in the day. Women in the late eighties and early nineties would often refer to themselves as a 'summer' or an 'autumn'. This idea that specific colours are for you while others are a no-go has regained popularity and has somehow gotten tangled up with colour psychology in the process. Not too long ago, I had a call with a prospective client who asked me to provide psychological evidence to support the 'fact' that people with pale skin shouldn't wear white.

'There *is* no research to support that,' I replied. 'At least, not to my knowledge.'

'But it's true; people with pale skin look terrible in white. They shouldn't wear it. They look like ghosts!'

'Well … that's one opinion. A subjective one, at that. Sorry, but I won't say that.'

Things got a bit awkward after that. Still, during that conversation, I finally understood my lecturer's issues with the perception of colour psychology and why they decided to ignore the discipline. Colour psychology explores how different colours make us feel and act, and also their impact on the way other people perceive us and behave towards us. As with make-up, we all believe that some clothing colours suit us more than others. A stylist or make-up artist might successfully pick colours that look great on you, but that's not colour psychology. Throw away any expectations you may have of me telling you what colour to wear to brighten your eyes or complement your skin's undertone. That's not my job. My job is to make you aware of scientific research that reveals the various ways in which colour brings an extra layer of meaning to your world – and, hopefully, to get you to wear more of it.

Colour outside the lines

> 'Colours are forces, radiant energies that affect us positively or negatively whether we are aware of it or not.'
>
> *Johannes Itten,* The Art of Color [1]

What's your favourite colour? It's a classic get-to-know you question that we've been asking since our days in the playground. Before we had the language to explain it, we had an acute awareness of the power of colour to shape our perceptions. We felt we had discovered a bit more about someone based on their response. Back then, a shared affinity for the colour green could have easily formed the basis of a blossoming friendship. But somewhere along the line, we all became shy. Colour became something to appreciate from afar rather than something to bond over, play with or invest in.

In 2021, I partnered with online personal styling service Stitch Fix UK to explore Brits' relationship with colour. The findings were illuminating. I was surprised to learn that seventy-nine per cent of people admit their wardrobe features primarily neutral colours such as black, grey and beige. What's more, only twenty per cent claimed to want to wear brighter colours and be braver with their fashion choices.[2]

An anthropological study conducted by a team of researchers from University College London shed further light on this neutral-palette obsession by observing women in the wild (read: shopping on a north London high street). In my head, I imagine a bunch of scientists scribbling on notepads behind a two-way mirror, saying things like: 'And if you look to your left, you'll find that the adult human female has rushed to pick up another black hoodie, despite owning three. Outstanding.'

Although it was probably less reminiscent of David Attenborough's *Planet Earth*, the results were equally fascinating. They found that most women will buy any piece of clothing 'as long as it's black'. Owning an all-black wardrobe wasn't something that happened to these women by accident, nor was it due to a shortage of colourful clothing options. People gravitate towards black because it's 'less individualising'. For these women, wearing black clothing gave them a heightened sense of security as it doesn't rock the boat, nor does it necessarily stand out from the crowd. Instead, they found that a more muted wardrobe helped them to blend in, which increased their chances of social acceptance.

It's undoubtedly true that brighter, more colourful outfits turn heads, drawing attention that can sometimes be unwanted. And we can all agree that putting together an all-black outfit is decidedly easier than figuring out if two or more colours go together. All in all, it's pretty common to feel more secure wearing all black. Nevertheless, brightening up your wardrobe comes with numerous benefits, such as the ability to enhance 'opportunities for creative expression'.[3] People just don't want to take the risk. But, as you'll understand by the end of this chapter, experimenting with colour is a risk worth taking. Before we get into all that, let me take you on a whirlwind tour of something you probably learned in year seven and have since forgotten: the science of colour.

Discovering the rainbow

The desire for a neutral wardrobe is a far cry from where we started. Scientists have traced our interest in colour as far back as 2600 BCE, when people first started dyeing their clothes, relying on vegetables, plants, animals and even insects to get the job done.[4] In ancient Egypt, medical professionals would give their patients a colour diagnosis in a practice called 'chromotherapy' which some people still engage in to this very day. Rather than write you a prescription for antibiotics, a doctor would instruct you to sit in a specifically coloured room to heal – as you can imagine, not a particularly reliable practice.

Colour plays an essential role in our day-to-day lives but no one really understood how it worked until Isaac Newton started messing around with light in the 1660s. Newton observed that when pure light enters a prism, it splits up – or 'refracts' – into an array of colours made up of different wavelengths. Warm colours, like red, orange and yellow, have longer wavelengths, while cooler colours, like blue, indigo and purple, have shorter wavelengths, with green sitting in the middle. The colours we see are what's being reflected back to us; the ones we don't see are absorbed by the object. For example, take a red shirt; it looks red because the dye molecules in the shirt's fabric have absorbed all of the light from the shorter end of the wavelength spectrum, while reflecting red light back to us.[5]

By delving a bit further into my GCSE physics textbook, I learned that we're actually capable of seeing 10 million shades of colour! To see light, our eyes rely on two different types of photoreceptors called rods and cones (I bet your lessons are coming back to you now). The rods are for night vision, while the cones are for high levels of light and colour.

There's a cone for long wavelengths (red), one for short wavelengths (blue) and one for those in between (green). The millions of colours that we can see are a result of our brains picking up signals from these three cones. These colour signals affect us physiologically, impacting our bodily functions, and psychologically, by delivering an emotional experience.[6]

If you gather a bunch of your friends and play a word association game with colour, it won't be long before you realise you're all saying the same things. You see red and think of passion or anger, while blue represents calmness or sadness. I'm right, aren't I? If I'm not, don't lose faith in me just yet, as I have an explanation – but first let me speak to the folks whose experience of colour is more universal.

Your body on colour

If you peel back the layers, you'll find that we're all pretty much the same underneath it all. No matter who you are or where you are in the world, our bodies typically function in the same way. If I tickle you, you'll laugh. If I step on your foot, you'll yell. Equally, research has consistently shown that our bodies react similarly to different colours. When faced with long-wavelength colours, like red, orange and yellow, our autonomic nervous system (ANS) becomes stimulated. The ANS regulates our blood vessels and internal organs, like the liver, stomach, heart and lungs. Each organ gets two different types of nerves from the ANS: sympathetic neurons, which increase bodily activity and help us make fight-or-flight responses, and parasympathetic neurons, which do the opposite, slowing down bodily activity and helping us to rest and digest.

The 'auto' in ANS refers to how this system enables our bodily functions to react automatically to everything in our environment, without our conscious awareness. Whether you find yourself gearing up to run a 10K or (more likely) chilling underneath a blanket, you know the ANS is involved in one way or another. The two parts work in harmony to ensure that your body responds appropriately at all times.

The mind–body connection suggests that your thoughts, attitudes, feelings and beliefs play an important role in your overall physical well-being. It's incredibly dynamic, but it's often the case that where the body goes, the mind follows. When you wear red, orange or yellow, your sympathetic system becomes activated. As a result, you feel more sociable, extroverted and energetic, because you're responding to your body telling you that it's time to get the party started. That's why long-wavelength colours are linked to more active emotions. On the other hand, short-wavelength colours have the opposite effect, activating the parasympathetic system and telling you to take it easy.

Fashion psychology tip

When gearing up for a big night in, choose a loungewear set or a pair of PJs in a short-wavelength colour. You're guaranteed to have a more peaceful evening wearing something blue than something red, because short-wavelength colours make us more relaxed.

Connecting the dots

Our bodily functions aren't the only things influencing our relationship with colour. Stephen Palmer and Karen Schloss's Ecological Valence Theory (EVT) also explains why specific colours evoke certain emotions and ideas.[7] When people see red, they think 'heart' or 'fire', while blue makes them think 'sea' or 'sky'. We've been exposed to these pairings without realising it for most of our lives. EVT argues that these pairings are so ingrained in us that they impact the emotions we experience when confronted with specific colours. You can use this reasoning to explain Stitch Fix UK's survey results.

Colour	Typical EVT pairing	Word association results
Yellow	sun	feeling optimistic (20 per cent)
Red	fire	feeling energetic (34 per cent)
Blue	sea	feeling calm (30 per cent)

The right-hand column features survey findings from research conducted by online personal styling service Stitch Fix UK. The percentages in brackets indicate the proportion of Brits surveyed who associated the emotion with each colour. Each emotion listed was the response given by the majority of respondents.

Take yellow as an example. People often associate it with the sun, something we Brits see around four times a year. But when we do see it, it's a cause for celebration: it's time to hang out in the park with friends and a couple of cans. These associations, which often occur unconsciously, cause us to feel optimistic when wearing yellow. You can apply this kind of reasoning with most colours.

Getting personal

'We see, in essence, not with two eyes but three:
with the two eyes of the body and with the eye of
the mind that is behind them. And it is in this eye of
the mind where the cultural-historical progressive
development of the colour sense takes place.'

Franz Delitzsch, theologian and Hebraist, 1878 [8]

EVT is a great way to predict which emotions you'll experience when wearing specific colours, but that's not where this story ends. A lot of OG colour psychologists believe that emotional responses to colour are universal, but personally, I think that's pushing it. You can't think of colour in such a rudimentary way when so many things can influence your experience of it. The best way to achieve a more nuanced relationship with colour is to consider the following four factors.

1. Your personal associations

Research has shown that colour-related emotions are incredibly dependent on personal preferences and people's past experiences with colour.[9] For example, I just explained why it's common for people to associate yellow with optimism. However, suppose you had an evil babysitter growing up, one who would force you to watch the news instead of cartoons and was famous for her signature yellow dresses. In that case, it's unlikely that you'll associate yellow with optimism. Frustration might be a more appropriate feeling.

Pink is often seen as a colour for little girls due to repeated exposure to marketing and advertisements that frame it as such. When you wear pink, you may feel playful and delicate – traits that are often stereotyped as belonging to young girls. To test this, a Japanese study investigated how men viewed themselves when wearing pink shirts. The researchers found that only men with low self-esteem felt that they exhibited more feminine traits when wearing pink,[10] suggesting that our internal belief system has the power to override certain colour stereotypes.

Take a moment to think about a colour to which you have a strong reaction. How have your personal experiences changed how you feel when wearing this colour, if you wear it at all?

2. Your cultural background

The colour of your outfit can change drastically in meaning depending on where you are in the world. In Texas, it's unlucky to get married in green, but in Ireland, it's good luck to wear green – especially on St Patrick's day.[11] In China, red is typically worn to big celebrations, as it's associated with happiness, good luck, and prosperity, while white is reserved for funerals. In the West, meanwhile, black is the colour of mourning, and white is more typically associated with weddings. In the States, Halloween is a major holiday, and the prevalence of orange pumpkins has caused many Americans to associate the colour with spooky festivities. Meanwhile, Buddhist monks are often seen wearing orange-coloured robes in South East Asia, so there, orange is considered a sacred and holy colour.

These cultural associations can shape your perception and preference for wearing specific colours, but these ideas become more fluid as we explore the world. One study found that Japanese people don't typically like dark red, while Americans do. Funnily enough, when Japanese students studied abroad in the US, they suddenly developed a preference for dark red.[12] There is some truth to the idea that we're all just products of our environment, after all.

3. Your language

In the English language, there are eleven key colours: red, orange, yellow, green, blue, purple, pink, brown, grey, black and white. But the way we speak about colours is anything but universal. In Korean, Vietnamese and Yoruba, people use one word for blue and green, often referencing the sky and grass to help differentiate. In Twi, a language spoken in Ghana, there are two words for purple: *beredum* and *afase-biri*. Different languages also have various colour-based idioms. In English, when someone is angry, we say 'they're seeing red', while a jealous person is 'green with envy'. The third Monday in January, considered the most depressing day of the year, is called 'Blue Monday', and the term 'purple prose' refers to overwrought writing. Your everyday conversations play a significant role in shaping the way you feel when wearing different colours.

4. Your age

When zooming in on older age groups, research has shown that forty per cent of those aged fifty-five to sixty and forty-four per cent of those over sixty-five were not afraid to wear brighter colours, stating that 'nothing stops them from embracing a colourful outfit', while just twenty-five per cent of younger people (aged eighteen to twenty-four) made the same claim.[13]

In the anthropological study mentioned earlier, we learned that some people prefer to wear neutral colours because they're considered more socially acceptable. All of my older friends and family members have told me that your capacity for giving an -ish about what's 'acceptable' slowly diminishes starting from age thirty. So, it might be the case that your inability to expand your colour palette has less to do with an emotional attachment to grey, beige and black, and more to do with the fact that you have yet to enter your 'I don't care' era. It'll come.

A colour breakdown

The capacity for colours to make us experience different emotions is dependent on the associations we give them. As I've explained, these associations depend on things like our biological tendencies, surroundings and lived experiences, and it's all too easy to get lost in the rainbow and wear something that gives off a different vibe than you intended. To alleviate this, I've made a simple summary of a tonne of colour psychology findings to give you a helping hand.

Red

Red carries a lot of connotations, but when it comes to clothing, red is considered the colour of champions. Its physiological effects make you better, faster and stronger. A study of the 2004 Olympics found that athletes wearing red won more events than those wearing blue.[14] The colour has been linked to success both in team sports[15] and in individual ones.[16] So you can go ahead and tell your *Fortnite*-obsessed nephew that they're more likely to win a multiplayer computer game when wearing red.[17] Psychologists suggest this effect is down to one of two things: red giving people more confidence, or red striking fear into the hearts of opponents.[18] That last part makes sense considering the fact that red makes people look more dominant and aggressive.[19]

Every Valentine's Day, clothing brands pull together edits of their best red 'fits and call it the colour of love, but it might be more accurate to call it the colour of lust. I'm always mildly disappointed to see Beyoncé's red dress get so little screen time in her 'Freakum Dress' video, because if you were to own a dress that screamed 'it's time to get it', it would come in red. Colour psychology research paints red as the colour of sexual power. Not only does red clothing appear to enhance our desirability,[20] it's also the winning lipstick shade if you want to meet someone at a bar.[21]

The best times to wear red

- when exercising
- when you need to be assertive
- when you want to get lucky after a hot date

Orange

Like red, orange makes us feel energetic and animated. It's generally considered to be a 'bright, happy and uplifting colour',[22] but it's one you won't often see when walking down the street. Given its substantial effect on the sympathetic nervous system, a head-to-toe orange look is inadvisable, as it can quickly become overwhelming. A 2018 study found that repeated exposure to the colour orange can make it harder for people to engage in tasks requiring concentration.[23] As our attention spans are often already hanging by a thread as it is, you should steer clear of orange when you're required to actually be an adult. Orange isn't for serious business; it's for fun. People associate it with playfulness and vibrancy, and consider it a welcoming and friendly colour.[24]

The best times to wear orange

- when you want to get in touch with your inner child
- when you want to stand out from the crowd
- when you want to boost your mood

Yellow

As highlighted by EVT, people generally consider yellow a happy colour, associating it with cheerful objects like sunshine and sunflowers. As a result, it evokes feelings of optimism and joy. When you're feeling shy or have to go to an event and meet a bunch of new people, it can often be easier to *wear* a conversation-starter rather than trying to start one yourself. If that's what you're aiming for, then try wearing yellow. Yellow grabs the attention (it's the most visible colour) and encourages feelings of extroversion and friendliness, helping you to step out of your comfort zone.[25]

Despite these positive associations, yellow is still a Marmite colour when it comes to clothing. When wearing yellow, you have to own it – or the colour will own you. For example, anecdotal evidence has found that in certain cases, yellow can cause you to experience negative emotions like frustration and annoyance. People tend to become more frustrated in yellow rooms, while overexposure to the colour can even make some people lose track of time.[26]

The best times to wear yellow

- when you want to make a memorable first impression
- when you want to get noticed
- when you want to encourage a more positive vibe

Pink

Women aren't inherently attracted to pink, and men aren't born fans of blue. Originally, pink was thought of as a masculine colour due to its similarity to red, which we know evokes feelings of dominance and power. In the 1940s, though, some marketing whiz made an arbitrary decision that pink was for girls, and everyone just went along with it.[27] Now, because pink has been repeatedly paired with products that we might see as feminine, wearing clothing in this colour will make you feel warm, nurtured and sincere. However, as I mentioned on page 64 when describing the study on how men feel when wearing pink shirts, this can change depending on how you see yourself.[28] Over time, gendered associations with pink have been impacted by the progression of feminism. As the movement heads into its fourth wave, many now associate pink with independence and power.[29]

The best times to wear pink

- when you feel playful
- when you want to connect to your femininity
- when you want to feel a sense of security

Green

As green sits right in the middle of the colour spectrum, it's often asso-ciated with balance. Depending on what type of person you are, green can be the colour of relaxation or motivation. For instance, people with a high need for achievement are more attracted to green.[30]

From an evolutionary perspective, it's easy to understand why green (or Marrs Green, to be precise) was listed as 'the world's favourite colour' in a 2017 global survey by British paper merchant G. F. Smith. Back in our hunter-gatherer days, green pointed to food, water and shelter – all of which were vital for survival.[31] Even if you've been stuck inside all day, staring at a screen, wearing green can remind you of the outdoors, help-ing you to relieve stress, think positively[32] and inspire creativity.[33] Green also has an 'optimism bias', a cognitive bias that has you feeling like a walking four-leaf clover,[34] so when you wear it, people are more likely to see you in a favourable light, as the colour allows you to exude positivity.

The best times to wear green

- when you feel boxed in
- when you have a tight deadline
- when you need to be creative

Blue

Blue is commonly associated with the sea and sky. If you've ever been on a beach holiday, you'll know that the mere sight of a clear sky and sprawling ocean is enough to quiet the mind. That's why blue is a great colour for relaxation. As I've mentioned, some languages have the same word for blue and green, and they're both considered to be calming colours. While blue is linked to positive beliefs, like communication, trust[35] and security,[36] in English it's also associated with sadness. Blue's ability to place us in a state of deep concentration can also make us overthink and subsequently 'feel blue'.

On the other hand, wearing blue can make you more efficient. It's been proven to reduce the number of errors people make by up to twenty per cent because it positively supports cognitive performance.[37] Blue's ability to sharpen your focus may explain why hiring managers consider it the best colour to wear to an interview.[38] But blue isn't just for worker bees; it also encourages people to innovate. In a pretty weird study, psychologists got participants to develop as many creative uses for a brick as they could in just one minute. When I tried this, I could not get past building a house or throwing it through an ex's car window (Jazmine Sullivan-style), but apparently that's because I didn't expose myself to blue. In the study, the participants exposed to blue came up with significantly more creative uses for a brick than those exposed to red.[39]

The best times to wear blue

- when you need to problem-solve
- when you need to self-soothe
- when you have a job interview

Purple

As purple has the shortest wavelength, it dramatically influences our parasympathetic nervous system and has a more prominent calming effect than blue or green. Shades like lavender have become synonymous with relaxation because purple lowers our blood pressure and heart rate and has a sedating effect on the body. Purple's ability to put us into an optimum state of relaxation makes it the perfect colour to wear when meditating, practising mindfulness or connecting with your spirituality. As such, it's associated with the supernatural and mystery, and also with feelings of comfort, security and peace.

Back in the day, purple was reserved for the aristocracy due to the rarity and cost of purple dye. While purple dye has since become much more affordable, it's still considered a luxurious, dignified and stately colour.[40] Purple can also feel like a considerably powerful colour for women, because along with green and white, it was adopted by the suffragettes as part of their movement in the early 1900s, when women fought for the right to vote.[41] Wearing the colour can bring these associations to the front of the mind and help wearers harness the strength displayed by those brave women.

The best times to wear purple

- when you want to connect to your spirituality
- when you want to alleviate feelings of insecurity
- when you want to feel luxurious

Grey

People consistently wear grey, even though it's rarely anyone's favourite colour. Every investigation into grey associates it with negative emotions. Unsurprisingly, people experiencing anxiety and depression typically use grey to represent their feelings.[42] It's not uncommon for people to favour grey loungewear pieces, but grey is also often considered to be a professional and formal colour. However, owning vast amounts of grey clothing should give you pause. You may want to question why you feel best represented by a colour usually associated with indifference and insecurity.

The best times to wear grey

- when you want to appear stoic or cool
- when you're running errands
- when you're lounging around at home

Brown

Brown is the colour of wood and earth, which is why it's related to things like seriousness,[43] reliability, support and dependability.[44] Pairing brown clothes with blue and green accessories will help you tap into these grounding emotions as a result of the earth–water correlation.

The fashion industry has had a problematic relationship with brown. When brown became nude, the colour was limited to lighter shades, making it nearly impossible for many people to find products like tights, underwear and even make-up that matched their skin tone. In 2017, I spoke to Ade Hassan, owner and founder of Nubian Skin, a lingerie and hosiery brand specialising in nude undergarments for women of colour. She told me: 'I remember in a trade show last year they were talking about trends, and one of the trends was "Different Skin Tones". I remember thinking, that's not a *trend*. We don't turn brown for the season and then turn back!'

As more designers like Ade redefine the meaning of 'nude', more inclusive shades of brown garments are becoming available. These increased offerings help people to celebrate and feel more confident in their own skin.

The best times to wear brown

- when you want to feel grounded
- when you want to appear more relatable
- when you want to celebrate your skin

Black

Like red, black is often associated with dominance, but in a more visceral way. A study investigating the performance of professional football and hockey teams discovered that players became more aggressive and received more disciplinary actions from referees when wearing black kits.[45] I even tested out this theory during the 2020 Euros, and much to my surprise, England won against Germany. Oh, and Germany, who were wearing black, committed more fouls. However, with the number of ciders I downed during the match, I wouldn't consider my findings particularly scientific.

Beyond the playing field, black clothing makes people feel power-ful – and others can sense it. Managers and those in senior positions are encouraged to wear black because studies have found that black clothes give you more influence in group situations.[46]

People don't just love to wear black due to its simplicity; in the right outfit, black can be anything but boring. It can ooze sophistication, glamour and stateliness, and, like deep shades of blue and purple, black can make you feel luxurious.[47] Its slimming powers are another reason why people are drawn to the colour; I'll go into more detail about that in Chapter 6.

The best times to wear black

- when you need to be particularly persuasive
- when you want to appear more authoritative
- when you're attending a glamorous event

White

We often associate white with a clean state, so when we wear it, we embody traits associated with purity, simplicity and peace.[48] A 2016 study discovered that people wearing white clothes consider themselves to be more moral, upstanding citizens than those wearing black.[49] When I think about white, Puff Daddy's famous all-white parties always spring to mind (yes, I'm of the age group that knew him as Puff Daddy), so I associate it with a wild time. However, studies suggest that I'm in the minority. White is ranked as the top colour for 'evoking moods of quiet-ness and concentration',[50] probably because you have to expend a tonne of mental effort trying to avoid getting dirty.

The best times to wear white

- when you need to be your best self
- if you ever find yourself on trial and need to profess your innocence (this is a tip for the genuinely innocent, mind you)
- when you need to clear your head

Don't forget the shades

All blues aren't the same. Different shades conjure different feelings, and that's something you need to factor in when utilising colour psychology. Studies have determined that the brightness of your clothing can be more important than facial expressions when people are making judgements about your capability.[51] Saturated and brighter colours are more arousing, but that doesn't necessarily mean bright is always best. Wearing darker shades can make people see you as competent because they allow you to appear more dominant.

Get to know your colours better

'We are the only species that can get a whole new
layer, and that is actually pretty amazing. We can

use colour like a magic wand, to boost how we feel,
wherever we are, whatever we are doing – and no
other creature does that!'

Karen Haller, The Little Book of Colour [52]

Now that you know practically everything there is to know about colour,
it's time to marry this up with your personal associations and tastes. My
'Embracing your rainbow' chart will help you discover the best way to
inject more colour into your wardrobe in a way that's unique to you. Before
you get your pencils out, commit to wearing all eleven colours this week.
Not all at once, mind you. No one's expecting you to go to work in a head-
to-toe yellow look. You can simply try to incorporate colourful accessories
or even underwear into your outfits: anything that will help you understand
how you may benefit from a broader colour palette. At the end of the week,
fill out the chart and reflect on your observations. I've used red here as an
example but please answer the questions for all eleven colours.

Embracing your rainbow

Questions	Colour: e.g. *Red*
What memories do you associate with this colour?	
What things do you most associate with this colour?	
What does this colour signify in your culture?	
What feelings do you associate with this colour?	

Questions	Colour: e.g. Red
How many clothes/ accessories do you own in this colour?	
When you wear this colour, how do you feel, physically and emotionally?	
How do people react to you when you wear this colour?	
How many times have you worn this colour this week?	
What other colours did you pair it with?	
Will you wear this colour again? Why/ Why not?	

As a society, we already confine our wardrobes to monotonous colour palettes, so try not to restrict yourself anymore by following silly colour rules. Go ahead and mix navy and black, and pair your silver jewellery with your gold pieces. If a colour pairing helps you successfully manage your emotions and navigate any situation that life may throw at you those little rules will appear incredibly insignificant. Later on, you'l discover how to implement this new-found knowledge to create a colour palette that works for your wardrobe.

Key takeaways

★ People gravitate towards muted colours because they're less individualising – they don't rock the boat and are generally considered easier to style. However, wearing a more expansive colour palette can allow you to embody the various positive traits that each colour brings.

★ Long-wavelength colours, like red, orange and yellow, activate sympathetic neurons in the autonomic nervous system (ANS), making you feel energetic and excited. Short-wavelength colours, like blue, indigo and purple, activate parasympathetic neurons in the ANS that help to calm you down.

★ Ecological valence theory (EVT) shows how the common associations we have with different colours affect the way we feel when wearing them.

★ While some colour associations are universal, you have to factor in your cultural background, language and personal associations in order to fully understand how your perceptions and feelings will change when wearing different colours.

Chapter 4

New look, who dis?

How clothes can make you think and act differently

'Each brand is selling you a curated identity,
and I absorb a bit of its essence when I put it
on – Eytys makes me feel edgy, Adanola makes
me feel sporty, Calvin Klein makes me feel
cool lounging around in my underwear – that's
marketing for you!'

Jessica Cheng, Creative and Art Director

People are always pretty confident about how they would react in a particular situation. You can say, 'I would have done this,' or 'That could never be me,' but the truth is, you never know what's going to happen until you're in the moment. So many of our actions are situation-dependent because we have to consider a host of different factors that can influence our behaviour: factors like the environment we're in, the people we're with and the clothes we're wearing. When you have a goal to achieve, it's easy to consider the clothes you're wearing as being relatively unimportant – but that couldn't be further from the truth.

Research has found that the clothes we wear have the power to change our thought processes and subsequent actions. It's a phenomenon called 'enclothed cognition' and the theory was introduced in a 2012 paper by psychologists Hajo Adam and Adam Galinsky. Enclothed cognition describes 'the systematic influence that clothes have on the wearer's psychological processes', and it's considered the bread and butter of fashion psychology.

In their study, Adam and Galinsky enlisted a group of participants to wear white coats. The group was then split in half. Group one was told their white coats were painters' smocks, worn by creatives for art projects. Group two were told they were wearing medical doctors' lab coats. Both groups were then tasked with two attention tests: a timed spot-the-difference task and a Stroop task (for example, seeing the word 'RED' written in blue font, and having to correctly identify the font colour without being confused by the text). The results revealed that when people believed they were wearing a doctor's coat, they scored significantly higher on the attention tests. Enclothed cognition works because, unbeknownst to us, certain clothes and outfits trigger our psychological schemas, bringing the symbolic meanings of clothes to the surface.[1]

Psychological schemas are cognitive frameworks or thought patterns that condense vast amounts of information and allow us to act appropriately in different situations based on prior knowledge. We possess different schema types, and our person-schemas include information about people, such as their behaviour, appearance, attitude and so on. Say you had a friend called Riley. Your person-schema for Riley might include ideas like 'stylish', 'hard-working' and 'sensitive'. Conversely, if I've only had bad experiences with Riley and have only seen that person at their worst, my person-schema could include descriptors like 'unkempt', 'brash' and 'loud'.[2] There's always room for individual differences with psychology, but, as we saw with colour, a good deal of our experiences are universal, causing us to develop similar schemas. It's pretty common to have a person-schema for a doctor that includes descriptions like 'methodical', 'attentive' and 'wears a white coat'. When we wear clothes that evoke these psychological schemas, we internalise or 'embody' them, and this comes out in the ways in which we think and behave.

With this study, Adam and Galinsky proved the existence of a mind–clothes connection, and chances are you've probably experienced this without realising it – but how can we harness the power of enclothed cognition for our own benefit? Perhaps you want to be a little more confident, more thoughtful or even more intelligent. There are a lot of things you can do to make this change, and it's important to exhaust all the tools at your disposal. Clothes are a criminally overlooked tool for self-transformation that can yield solid results.

At the start of this journey, I explained how your clothes impact the different ways in which you view yourself, one of them being the person you hope to be. That person may seem completely out of your reach, but your clothes can act as a ladder to help you bridge the gap if you know how to use them correctly. In this chapter, I will guide you through studies that outline the different ways in which clothes and accessories can transform the behaviour of their wearers, and show you how you can take advantage of this knowledge. Some may be obvious, others less so, but all of them will make you more cognisant of the way your attitude shifts depending on what you have on. Towards the end of the chapter,

I'll account for the differences in our psychological schemas by showing you how you can create a personalised enclothed cognition framework.

How to dress to . . . think bigger

Earlier, I revealed how tailored suits and other formal-wear pieces make people perceive you as powerful, but perception isn't everything. Studies have shown that people tend to desire a type of power that gives them autonomy rather than a type of power that gives them influence over others.[3] One way to gain autonomy is to think in unconventional ways that make you stand out from the crowd, and formal wear allows you to do just that.

In a 2015 study published in the journal of *Social Psychological and Personality Science*, researchers investigated the impact of clothing on the thought process of college students. The students were interviewed and made self-judgements about how formally they were dressed in relation to other students passing by. Once they'd made these judgements, they completed a behavioural identification form to provide researchers with a deeper insight into the way they thought about themselves. The results revealed that those who considered themselves to be more formally dressed than their peers were able to adopt a 'better holistic view' of the world. They were more likely to engage in abstract thinking, which essentially means they were able to see the bigger picture. Surprisingly, researchers concluded that these formally dressed students were also more likely to reach their long-term goals.[4] It's not uncommon for people to fear being overdressed in any given situation, but it may enable you to expand your current way of thinking and open you up to new possibilities.

Formal clothing doesn't only change the way you think; it changes the way you talk. When people were asked to describe themselves, psychologists uncovered that those dressed casually tended to use words like 'easy-going' and 'nonchalant'. On the other hand, some of the adjectives used for more formally dressed people included words like 'strategic', 'neat' and 'tolerant'.[5] Self-talk is incredibly important because it can alter the way you see yourself and your capabilities, which subsequently affects your behaviour. If you're describing yourself as someone who 'goes with the flow' when circumstances call for you to be more 'strategic', chances are there's going to be some disappointment on the horizon. Whether you're a fan of formal clothing or prefer to be more laid-back, it's incredibly important to consider how your clothes influence the way you see yourself.

Fashion psychology tip

Don't neglect your undies. Just because they're hidden, doesn't mean they won't have an effect on your behaviour. A lot of talk around underwear is binary: it's either seen as functional or sexy. Your underwear doesn't have to be so limiting if you develop a schema that associates it with different traits. Making your pants an afterthought could stop you from experiencing the power of enclothed cognition in whatever outfit you're wearing on top.

How to dress to . . . be meticulous

I've always admired meticulous people. The people that triple-check everything and can spot even the most minuscule of flaws. I've always been more of a 'close-enough' person. At times, this has worked in my favour, but it's also been known to bite me in the butt. You couldn't imagine my joy when, during my research, I discovered that you can accessorise your way to meticulousness.

A study by psychologists David Ellis and Rob Jenkins investigated the actions of watch-wearers.[6] They asked a group of participants to attend a scheduled appointment, and discovered that those who wore a watch arrived significantly earlier to appointments than watch-less people. You may be thinking, 'Well, duh. Of course, seeing the time will make you *be* on time.' But these days, most watch-wearers don't constantly check their watch. In fact, it's more of a reflex to glance at your phone to check the time, regardless of whether or not you're wearing a watch.

Ellis and Jenkins found that the ability to check their watches had nothing to do with the participants' arrival time. Rather, we've developed a positive schema of watch-wearers that impacts the way we behave: 'Choosing to wear a watch appears to act as a social marker for an individual who is likely to be more conscientious.' Being conscientious doesn't just mean you have your -ish together; it means you're more organised, more diligent and generally more meticulous. Researchers argued that even if you're going to be late for something, wearing a watch influences you to be 'dutiful enough to try to limit your lateness'.

Reaching for your Casio may not be the first thing you think of when you're feeling all over the place, but according to the research, it may help you embrace the prudent traits of watch-wearers. The change may be subtle, but it's an easy action to take and the reward will certainly outweigh the effort.

More so than clothes, accessories are drenched in symbolism, so they constitute a powerful force when it comes to enclothed cognition. Have you ever noticed the movie trope of very intelligent characters wearing specs? Interestingly, evidence suggests there's a strong correlation between high levels of intelligence and needing to wear glasses.[7] For the sight-challenged among us, if you want to feel smarter, perhaps it's time to ditch the contact lenses and make a trip to Specsavers.

Fashion psychology tip

Watches with larger faces draw more attention due to their size and feel. Being more conscious of your watch is likely to increase your predisposition towards embodying conscientiousness.

How to dress to . . . be fitter

One of the first things to go out the window when you become stuck in a rut is your fitness routine. We all know how important exercising is to help us stay healthy and live longer. We also know that exercising is a natural mood-booster – but building up enough motivation to get going in the first place can be challenging. Especially if, like me, you suffer from second-hand tiredness. It's a medical condition I invented to explain the feeling of exhaustion after merely watching other people going on those early-morning runs. 'Good for them,' I'd think, as I sluggishly tucked into my double sausage and egg McMuffin.

How did I break free from that endless cycle of 'I'll start tomorrow'? I updated my collection of workout gear.

The style of your workout gear can cause your body to trick your mind into thinking you want to work out. Throughout the chapter on colour psychology, I identified the physiological impact colour has on us. Workout gear in long-wavelength colours like red and orange is great, as these colours activate our autonomic nervous system and give us more energy. However, when utilising colour psychology to change your behaviour, you have to consider the hue and brightness of the colours you're wearing. Saturated and brighter colours are more rousing and will give you more energy, while deep and dull colours have been found to induce tiredness. The next time you fall out of your healthy habits, try to incorporate activewear in bold and bright hues into your weekly outfits; this will allow you to tap into a more active mindset and reach your fitness goals.[8, 9]

How to dress to . . . be selfish

Enclothed cognition isn't all sunshine and rainbows. Some research has revealed that in occasional obscure cases, clothes can bring out divisive and unfavourable traits. A study investigating the link between luxury goods and political attitudes found that carrying luxury handbags can cause people to express more conservative political views, particularly when it comes to money. This shift occurred because it's common to develop a psychological schema of luxury-goods owners as being more close-fisted. The research also found that carrying a luxury bag reduced the wearers' capacity for self-control and made them less generous.[10] Big 'let them eat cake' energy.

While not specific to selfishness, this next study highlights how clothes can cultivate harmful thought patterns. For a study published in the *Journal of Personality and Social Psychology*, researchers enlisted a group of women to complete a series of maths tests. The women were split into two groups, with one group completing the test in a sweater and the other group in a swimsuit. Despite there being no difference in the average intelligence of the two groups, the women wearing the swimsuits performed significantly worse than those wearing sweaters. The swimsuits caused participants to experience 'self-objectification', where you embody negative schemas. In this instance, the schema was that women who wear revealing clothes are uneducated.[11]

The dark side of enclothed cognition

'A hoe never gets cold.'

Cardi B

The world may think of Cardi B as a superstar rapper, but I consider her to be something of a budding fashion psychologist. When she uttered the phrase above in a now-viral video, she made a pretty astute observation. In a 2021 study, researchers from the University of South Florida wanted to test the hypothesis that looking 'hot' stops you from literally feeling cold. The researchers interviewed a series of women wearing their best freakum dresses outside a club on an extremely cold night out. They discovered that women who engaged in self-objectification reportedly felt less cold than women with low self-objectification.[12] While taking pride in your appearance can be empowering, it's dangerous to have your self-worth so closely aligned with your physical appearance, as this can dehumanise you to the point where you become disconnected from your feelings, both emotionally and, in this case, physically. Rather than getting rid of your risqué clothes (I certainly won't be), you should evaluate the schema you have of people who dress in this manner. Do you find yourself unconsciously making stereotypically negative judgements about the morals, behaviour and ethics of people who dress in revealing outfits? By addressing this bias and changing the way you think, you can avoid experiencing the weird consequences of self-objectification. You will, however, need to invest in a warm going-out coat.

After you get dressed, you must take a moment to really consider whether you'll spend the day worrying about what other people think. It would be easy for me to tell you to stop worrying, but being judged is unavoidable, and we all care about what other people think of us. Social cognitive neuroscience has revealed that a number of brain areas are consistently activated and cause us to constantly consider our relationship with others; how we interact, co-operate and even compete with other people.[13] If you're not confident about the meanings you attribute to certain clothes, you'll be easily swayed by harmful and outdated stereotypes that will negatively affect your mindset. These studies may seem a little extreme, but they stress why your everyday clothing decisions should never be an afterthought. If you don't make the effort to consider the psychological schemas that your outfit evokes, you won't realise how your outfit affects you, and the way you treat yourself and others.

For me, wearing revealing clothes evokes a schema of the powerful artists and entertainers I wanted to be when I grew up, but another person's schema of power can look entirely different. That's why it's important to build a wardrobe that incorporates your personal psychological schemas and allows you to experience the full benefits of enclothed cognition.

Three steps to enclothed cognition

Step one: Determine what [insert specific trait] looks like to you

In the fashion design competition show *Project Runway*, the designers are always asked to paint a full picture of their look. They're asked to explain their look and answer questions like 'What does your model do?', 'Where are they going?' and 'How are they feeling?'. These questions serve to imbue the outfit with symbolism and create a psychological schema. I want you to do the same thing – but start backwards. Think about a trait you want to embody, like power, fitness or romance. Next, create an online visual board of all the clothes and accessories that spring to mind when you think about this trait.

Step two: Identify the people you associate with [insert specific trait]

In 2014, psychologist Karen Pine found that when people wore a Superman T-shirt, the heroic emblem changed their views of their own abilities. The effect of enclothed cognition caused them to confidently assume they possessed some of Superman's super-strength. They believed they could physically lift heavier weights simply because they were wearing something symbolic of strength. Now, certain traits are bound to conjure up images of people whose style doesn't appeal to you. As much as you may want to embody strength and resilience, it's unlikely that you'll want to emulate Clark Kent's alter-ego wardrobe in your day-to-day life.

Spend some time creating a new visual board, this time of people who embody your desired trait *and* possess a style you admire. This will help you rework the schemas you have for this specific trait. The people you choose don't have to be famous; they could be anyone, even people you know on a personal level. Now, identify the clothes and accessories they wear that appeal to you most and add them to the board you created in step one.

Step 3: Solidify your psychological schema

In another experiment featured in Adam and Galinsky's ground-breaking paper, participants were asked to write an essay about how they identified with the white coat (for example, how the coat represented them and the personal meaning it evoked). This exercise was intended to solidify the symbolic meaning of the coats to ensure that wearers experienced enclothed cognition.[14] Put together an outfit made up of pieces you already own that resemble those featured in the visual board you've created. When you have the outfit on, stand in front of the mirror and engage in a mini mindfulness exercise. Conjure up scenarios and descriptive words that you associate with the trait you're trying to embody; you can even say them out loud if you feel comfortable doing so. This practice will serve to solidify your mind–clothes connection and increase the likelihood of you experiencing enclothed cognition when wearing this outfit.

Repeat these three steps for the different traits you wish to embody.

It's OK to take your style cues from fashionistas or stylists, but you'll see a greater shift in your behaviour if you dress according to your personal psychological schema. How you connect the dots between clothing styles and traits hinges on the experiences and beliefs that are unique to you. If you consider a sock to be lucky, you'll embody that winning feeling every time you slip it on. If you consider your Bridget Jones-style knickers to be sexy, sultriness will ooze out of you with one snap of the waistband. Dressing in this way will take you from 'woe is me' to 'new look, who dis?'.

Key takeaways

★ The theory of enclothed cognition reveals that clothes have the power to change the ways in which we think and behave. Embracing enclothed cognition involves applying a layer of symbolism to your outfits.

★ We often associate a specific person and/or specific character traits with certain clothing styles. Subsequently, when we wear these styles, we embody those traits.

★ If you want to change the way you feel when wearing a particular style, you must first address the judgements you make about people you commonly associate with those styles.

Chapter 5

Wearapy

How to tap in to the protective power of style

'If you look good, you feel good, and if you feel good, you play good.'

Deion Sanders

Experiencing a boost in your mood when you take care of your appearance is not a new concept. I've been dropping psychology studies and research throughout this book to support this well-known fact, but now it's time to take things a step further. Some of the literature surrounding the concept of mood-dressing is incredibly binary – you're either dressed for distress or for joy – but it's not that simple. Allow me to introduce you to a new concept called 'wearapy'. Wearapy is the practice of using clothes to help boost your mood, confront your feelings and successfully navigate different emotional states.

When it comes to wearapy, people always ask whether it's more important to dress in a way that reflects how they feel in the moment, or in a
way that reflects how they *want* to feel. And the answer depends on your
personal desires. Dressing how you currently feel helps you to stay present
by honouring your state of mind. Dressing how you want to feel gives
you the power to shift your mood and potentially take you out of negative emotional states. The act of dressing to honour or alter your mood
is wearapy. The subsequent emotional experience and mood change is a
type of enclothed cognition, as explored in the previous chapter.

A global survey investigating the mood-altering effects of clothing
revealed that clothes don't simply make people feel 'good' – forty-two per
cent of respondents believed that certain outfit choices made them feel
more relaxed.[1] I've dubbed this 'GABA-dressing', because when we wear
these relaxing outfits, they foster the release of gamma-aminobutyric
acid (or GABA) neurotransmitters (chemical messengers) in the brain.
When attached to proteins known as GABA receptors, these produce a
calming and relaxing effect on the body.[2] Meanwhile, forty per cent of
people admitted that clothes have the power to make them feel confident.[3] This is what we can call 'serotonin-dressing' (serotonin being the
neurotransmitter that plays a critical role in confidence).[4] A separate UK
study found that more than two-thirds of Brits believe that the way they
dress can boost their moods and make them feel better about themselves
(more on 'dopamine-dressing' shortly). Thirty-five per cent of people also
stated that they felt a day or situation had gone better than anticipated
because of their clothes. Survey data has found that over ninety-six per
cent of people 'reported a change in their emotional state with a change
in their style of dressing'.[5]

Absolutely anyone can tap into the mood-altering benefits of clothing.
However, research investigating binary gender differences in wearapy

suggests that because women are socialised to be highly invested in their personal style, they have a stronger emotional connection to clothes than men.[6] When women choose outfits, it tends to be based on how something makes them feel. Women are also more likely to be walking mood rings, matching their outfits to their moods, especially when feeling confident, happy and empowered. In his research, Dr Alastair Tombs, senior marketing lecturer at the University of Queensland's business school, asserted that women use clothes as a tool of self-expression, both to showcase and manage their moods, and generally have a stronger emotional attachment to clothing.[7]

Given these overwhelming findings, it's annoying, to say the least, that those who identify as women are regularly chastised for being 'too invested' in fashion. Sometimes, if a woman is seen as putting effort into her personal style, her intelligence and capabilities are questioned, as if we cannot possibly be both accomplished and style-conscious. This trope is especially true when it comes to political figures. When a woman in politics gets media attention, it's a toss-up between how much attention will be paid to her policies and how much will be paid to her looks. It tends to swing towards the latter. Take British politics, for example: if you search 'Theresa May outfits' on Google, you'll see just over six million results, but type in 'Boris Johnson outfits' and the number of hits will decrease by thirty-seven per cent. Neither politician is considered a style icon, but the amount of attention given to May's kitten heels during her tenure was over the top. As I revealed in Chapter 2, utilising your clothing as a tool for impression management is an excellent way of gaining more control over your narrative. Still, various factors like prejudices and social norms don't always make this easy. Dressing according to wearapy provides you with a greater sense of personal control.

In the previous chapter, you learned how to harness the power of enclothed cognition, but what does a combination of wearapy and enclothed cognition look like in the wild? In this chapter, I want to take you from psychological concept to reality. I'll provide you with seven simple rules to show you how easy it is to incorporate these ideas into your everyday life.

The dos and don'ts of wearapy

1. DO switch it up

I've never been one for signature styles. I'm even less fond of so-called 'style tribes'. Dressing according to wearapy means being in tune with your feelings. No one's mood is the same every day, so why should your clothes be uniform? Fashion legends like Anna Wintour and Karl Lagerfeld are known for their unwavering looks, but outside of this high-fashion bubble, having a signature style can be incredibly limiting.

With anything in life, too much of one thing isn't good, and fashion psychology reveals that your clothes are no different. Do Something Different is the UK-based company behind the Flex app, a behaviour-change system designed to build well-being by helping you track and address your behaviours, thoughts and feelings.[8] As part of their initiative, they hosted a 'Wear Something Different' programme that encouraged attendees to shake up their wardrobe habits and revamp their looks. The programme was tailored to each individual, so if someone wore a lot of denim, they were encouraged to introduce different fabrics into their wardrobe. If they only owned plain grey socks, they were advised to jazz it up and broaden their colour palette. Feedback from attendees also showed that these small changes made a huge difference to their overall well-being, with seventy-three per cent of people reporting reduced anxiety, while eighty-two per cent felt that their stress levels fell as a result of implementing these simple wardrobe changes.[9]

Some days I feel delicate, and I lean in to that feeling by wearing maxi dresses in soft fabrics. Other days I feel frail, and I'll choose to move out of that emotion by wearing corset tops, tailored trousers and other pieces I associate with me at my strongest. If I had the wardrobe of a cartoon character and was forced to wear the same outfit over and over, I wouldn't be able to make this shift, which would leave me feeling repressed.

2. DON'T overdo it

Psychologists have been known to infer changes in their patients' moods from changes in their appearance both positive and negative. While it's often the case that a dishevelled appearance is indicative of a low mood, many people don't realise that placing too much emphasis on your appearance is also a worrying sign. Perfection is a myth. Putting pressure on yourself to look perfect fosters anxiety that directly counteracts any positive benefits you can get from wearapy. You could wear one hell of a power outfit, but you wouldn't be able to embody power if you then waste energy obsessing over something petty like wrinkles on your shirt. A slight wrinkle never harmed anyone, but anxiety can have a huge impact.

If you feel overly concerned about your appearance, do the work to uncover what's happening beneath the surface. This work could include anything from journaling to meditation and therapy. You're more likely to develop an unhealthy obsession with your appearance when you place too much emphasis on external perceptions. Yes, clothes can give you the power to successfully manage what people think about you, but if you're becoming consumed by this it's time to make wearapy more of a priority instead.

3. DO dopamine-dress

When people think of wearapy, dopamine-dressing is often the first thing that comes to mind because it provides psychological grounding to the 'look good, feel good' concept. Dopamine-dressing is the act of wearing something that you associate with happiness, allowing you to subsequently embody that positive emotion. The happiness you feel from dopamine-dressing stems from the chemical dopamine, which mediates pleasure in the brain. It occurs in the ventral tegmental area (VTA), which is located in the midbrain and is an integral part of the brain's reward system. From there, dopamine is released into the nucleus accumbens – 'the neural interface between motivation and action'[10] – and the prefrontal cortex – the area of the brain that is linked to attention, memory and our ability to think flexibly.[11] You already know how to dopamine-dress, because it's simply a type of enclothed cognition that's connected explicitly to happiness. Take the framework laid out on pages 91–92 and use the word 'happiness'. You might even want to place these happiness-inducing outfits in a particular spot in your wardrobe to allow you to easily reach for them when you're feeling low.

4. DON'T save your favourites for a special occasion

Playing dress-up is not just for kids. Wearing clothes that offer some respite from the hustle and bustle of everyday life allows you to leave your to-do list and anxieties behind, even if it's just for a few hours. Dressing up is a type of wearapy because outlandish clothes carry a 'tension release dimension'[12] that fosters a feeling of escapism.

I've never been on board with the whole 'saving your favourite clothes for a special occasion' thing, probably because I wasn't brought up that way. I have distinct childhood memories of going shopping with my dad and trying on clothes as he waited nearby for the thumbs-up or -down. If something got a thumbs-up, rather than having me change back into my own clothes, he'd rip off the tag, hand it to the cashier and pay. I always loved strutting out of shops dripping in fresh swag. I was so happy, I barely acknowledged the way my mum would make a fuss about me potentially ruining my 'good-good clothes' before I had a chance to wear them to something special. Being the terror that I was, I pushed and pushed until she let me model my favourite pieces around the house on weekends. When I wore these coveted items, I felt special, and although I didn't know it at the time, those regular Saturdays became special occasions in their own right simply because I dressed as if they were.

Research shows that when we wear our favourite pieces, they help us control our emotions, foster a sense of togetherness and even make us feel more outgoing.[13] If we experience all of these great things when wearing our favourite clothes, then why should we save them for a specific day?

5. DO honour your culture

Embracing Afro-diasporic styles and purchasing from Black-owned brands boosts my mood, as it's a way for me to celebrate my cultural identity. Sadly, when growing up as an ethnic minority, it can feel like you're constantly pressured to assimilate. Cultural assimilation is defined as 'the process in which a minority group or culture comes to resemble a society's majority group'[14] and it's encouraged via the constant devaluation and appropriation of culturally significant styles. Cultural appropriation is 'the unacknowledged or inappropriate adoption of the customs, practices, ideas, etc. of one people or society by members of another and typically more dominant people or society',[15] and there are countless examples of this happening in fashion.

Major fashion houses have been known to steal from smaller ethnic minority designers, and styles are often labelled 'ghetto' when worn by their originators and 'high fashion' when they're stolen. These actions serve to diminish the self-concept of ethnic minorities – the idea we have about ourselves that's constructed from our internal beliefs and reactions from others.[16] It can leave us questioning where we fit in, and in some cases can cause us to distance ourselves from our culture.

When writing for my blog *Fashion is Psychology*, Sabrina Cheema, a British-Asian personal stylist, explained how confusing it can feel to experience this disconnect. 'As a creative, I have a great appreciation for the rich beauty of South Asian clothing, yet the thought of putting one of those outfits on can often fill me with dread. This feeling of disconnect has dazed me for many years because surely, one would assume that I would feel more comfortable in my ethnic clothing than those of the Western world.'[17] If, like Sabrina, you want to make stylistic changes to your wardrobe to incorporate your culture, you can feel comforted in the knowledge that cultural dressing has a proven positive impact on your mental well-being.

To investigate the intersection between clothing and cultural identity, researchers at Queen Mary University conducted a longitudinal study (one that takes place over a really long time) on Bangladeshi teenagers.[18] The results revealed that the teens who regularly wore their traditional style of dress 'were less likely to have later mental health problems' than those who shied away from cultural clothing. These findings probably occurred because embracing your cultural style allows you to embrace a major part of your identity and all the positive things you associate with it. When you embrace your culture in such a way, you're grounding yourself by fostering a sense of belonging. It's therefore important to create more opportunities to celebrate your cultural background through your style, even in small ways.

6. DON'T dismiss the squeeze

If you've ever tried swaddling a baby, you'll know that it's a countdown to sleepy town once that last bit of fabric is tucked in. Swaddling is an easy trick to soothe miserable babies – but can it soothe miserable adults? Scientists have discovered that 'deep-touch pressure' – or a squeezing sensation around the body – has therapeutic and calming effects. We're all prone to drowning our bodies in oversized clothing when we're feeling low, but research suggests that we might be taking the wrong approach if we're looking for a mood boost. Activewear, compression wear and even form-fitting clothing in general can allow you to experience deep-touch pressure and the accompanying anxiety-reducing benefits.[19] Think of these garments as movable weighted blankets: a little bit of pressure with a big reward.

7. DO embrace nostalgia

'Ahh, the good old days.'

That saying is the reason why everything always seems to be 'making a comeback', why the nineties will never die and why Disney won't ever stop doing remakes. The current socio-political landscape makes it seem like there are more things that divide us than bring us together. However, one thing we all share, no matter our style, age, gender or ethnicity, is a love of nostalgia – a sentimental longing for the past that continues to make everything, including fashion, circular. Next time you consider getting rid of an 'out-of-style' outfit, remember you might be throwing away a chance to experience wearapy and embody the positive psychological effects of nostalgia.

Nostalgia protects your mental well-being.[20] After engaging in nostalgia-inducing activities, research has shown that people:

- experience higher self-esteem
- are more optimistic
- feel less lonely
- feel more socially connected
- are more creative
- feel cosier!

It's true, triggering nostalgia can even change the way we experience the elements. A 2012 study found that when people were placed in cold rooms, taking a trip down memory lane made them feel warmer.[21] Looking back at your life through old, rose-coloured glasses can make you feel good, but wearing them can make you feel even better. Clothes are like memory banks; they constitute a powerful tool that can trigger nostalgia, which in turn breeds happiness and lifts your mood. And to be honest, nothing ever truly goes out of style. If a garment gives you the ability to hark back to the good old days, cherish it for a little while longer.

These seven points constitute the main principles of wearapy. If you consider these principles every day, you won't simply be getting dressed, you'll be engaging in an act of self-care. Despite the conveniences of modern-day life, none of us are immune to its many stressors. Think of your clothes as the first line of defence: tools that not only help you regulate your mood, but boost it as well. As a fashion psychologist, I have keen insight into the impact of clothes on our mental well-being. I've done the research and I know the theories like the back of my hand, but it wasn't until I went through one of the most challenging periods of my life that I gained an in-depth appreciation for the power of clothing.

Dealing with grief, one outfit at a time

> 'In a way, inherited fashion is like mourning itself. Your memories and grief are knitted together like the yarns of a woollen jumper. You wear it on your body until it becomes a part of you.'
>
> *Marjolijn Oostermeijer* [22]

You don't realise the importance of possessions until someone's gone.

When I lost my sister to cancer, my world turned upside down. An eight-year age gap meant nothing to us; we were as inseparable as identical twins. Our bond grew stronger with each passing year. We lived together, we hung out together, we shared most things. Arguments were fleeting, because sharing a joke was more important than being right. I'm not going to lie, wrapping my head around this type of permanency has been tough, to say the least.

The whole thing was doubly traumatic because we didn't realise what was going on until it was too late. One minute we're ringing in the new year in a club in central London; the next minute, we're in the ICU. Sometimes I think that if I'd had a chance to prepare myself, things might have been easier – but if you've ever lost someone, you know that nothing can prepare you for the debilitating pain that ensues. I became a 'Munty' overnight – not quite a mum, but more than an aunty – to my darling niece and nephew.

Losing an adult sibling puts you in a very weird position. Your parents have lost a child, your niece and nephew have lost a mother, and you're kind of somewhere in the middle, trying to hold everyone together. I didn't 'deal' with the grief at first. I jumped into a new relationship and a new career, and thought that if I just acted like everything was alright, then it would be.

It wasn't.

When both the relationship and the job fizzled out, I realised that you can't run from grief, as there's simply nowhere to hide. You have to go through it – and keep going – because, as sad as it is, life stops for no one, not even for the brilliant, beautiful and kind person I had the pleasure of sharing a lifetime with.

There is no one-size-fits-all solution for dealing with loss. While my mother has relied on her faith, I've noticed that things get a little easier for me when I'm in the presence of my sister's belongings. Our love of fashion was one of the many things we bonded over. As with most sibling relationships, when it came to clothes and accessories, the concept of ownership changed daily. Her old jumpsuit slowly became our jumpsuit; my new top instantly became hers upon the joint conclusion that she looked better in it. We constantly went back and forth like this, dipping into each other's wardrobes whenever we saw fit. I would even find myself wearing the woman's maternity dresses, passing them off as oversized. Hey, when it works, it works.

Over time, the contents of our wardrobes became a part of our shared identity. Now that she's gone, I've realised how clothes are truly an extension of yourself – and how your selfhood is weaved into the fabric of every garment you wear. The medial prefrontal cortex is an area of the brain that activates when you're thinking about yourself, and studies show that this area also activates when we 'create associations between external things and ourselves through ownership'.[23] What this means is that our clothes are very much part of who we are, and they conjure up countless narratives of both our singular and collective identities. After my sister passed, every time I clung to her clothes, I was engaging in wearapy. When looking at pictures became too overwhelming, these outfits acted as a portal to keep me connected to my sister and channel our happy memories. They were a much-needed source of comfort.

Every culture and generation has its traditions surrounding the use of clothes to symbolise and process loss. In Edwardian-era Britain, the length of time for which a woman wore mourning clothing would depend on how close she was to the departed: a widow would dress in mourning for two years, while a woman who had lost a parent or child would do so for one year. Over in the States, in the late 1800s, widows wore mourning clothing for two years or more, while losing a parent meant you wore them for one year, and a sibling just six months.[24]

I passed the six-month mark a long time ago, but I've worn the dress I wore to my sister's funeral on several occasions since. As clothes can act as a time capsule, some people would find it too traumatic to even look at their funeral outfit, let alone wear it. When speaking to my best friend Alysha, who sadly lost her mother to breast cancer three years prior, she agreed. She felt that clothes worn on such sad occasions were 'tainted'. Our difference of opinion underscores the different ways in which grief affects us all. For me, because I was in a state of shock and denial for such a long time, I needed a tangible reminder of my pain. Wearing the dress again helped me to confront my grief. It provided me with a physical connection to the abstract pain of my loss. It was also a reminder that I had been through the worst that life had thrown at me so far, and somehow I'd managed to come out the other side.

Fashion psychology tip

Use your clothes as a memory box. If you've lost a loved one, think back to a happy moment you shared. What were you wearing? Use that outfit as a way to help you stay connected to the good times. Every time you wear it, you're transporting yourself back to those happy moments.

Everyone deals with trauma in their own way, but there are many ways in which clothes can help you get through trying times. Like me, you can use them as a way to help you acknowledge your pain. You can also use your clothes to embody the good times, to celebrate your identity, and to remind you of the person you used to be when you become disconnected to yourself. You can even use clothes to help you realise how far you've come, and to cultivate a new identity as you navigate your new reality. Life is hard enough as it is, so don't waste a valuable asset, especially one that is always at your disposal. Practise wearapy and watch as things start to become that little bit easier.

Key takeaways

★ In the busyness of everyday life, it can become difficult to tap in to our emotions, but our clothes may provide the solution. Wearapy is the practice of using clothes to help boost your mood, confront your feelings and successfully navigate different emotional states.

★ GABA-dressing is a type of wearapy that focuses on relaxation.

★ Serotonin-dressing is a type of wearapy that focuses on confidence.

★ Dopamine-dressing is a type of wearapy that focuses on embracing positive emotional states.

★ You can practise wearapy by forgoing signature styles and switching up your outfits, embracing cultural clothes and accessories, regularly wearing your favourite pieces and making comfort a priority.

★ Nostalgia dressing is another type of wearapy that involves wearing clothes that evoke sentimental memories of the past. It's often considered a great way to tackle challenging emotions like grief.

Chapter 6

_____

Well, you can't be naked

Exploring the dynamic relationship between clothes and the body

'This body had carried me through a hard life. It looked exactly the way it was supposed to.'

Veronica Roth, Carve the Mark

When we talk about the body, in any capacity, it simply doesn't make sense to exclude clothing from the conversation. As I mentioned in the introduction, society has yet to evolve to the point of accepting public nudity, so for the time being, our bodies spend more time clothed than they do unclothed. In *The Fashioned Body*, Joanne Entwistle beautifully describes clothes as 'the meeting place of the private and public'. I'm obsessed with this concept because it underscores the importance of viewing your style choices as a profoundly personal experience. The relationship we have with our bodies is dynamic. Still, many people don't realise that when clothes facilitate this 'meeting', it causes a ripple effect in your self-concept – the way you see yourself and the way others see you.

If you're still having trouble understanding how your clothes do more than simply conceal or reveal different parts of your body, consider the following:

- Have your feelings about your body ever affected the styles you wear?
- Have your clothes ever changed the way you feel about your body?
- Have you ever had to change your personal style to better accommodate your body?

Most people will answer yes to at least one, if not all, of these questions at some point in their lives. I'm three for three. Sometimes, these feelings can extend beyond our bodies and self-concept and even change how we view our position in the world. So, when you're discussing the body, you really ought to consider the *clothed (or fashioned)* body. Entwistle's research shows that clothes act as a tool, giving our body meaning and helping to shape our identity.[1] She writes:

Dress is the way in which individuals learn to live in their bodies and feel at home in them. Wearing the right clothes and looking our best, we feel at ease with our bodies, and the opposite is equally true: turning up for a situation inappropriately dressed, we feel awkward, out of place and vulnerable. In this respect, dress is both an intimate experience of the body and a public presentation of it.[2]

This chapter will highlight how clothes impact your body image – and vice versa. I'll discuss how Western beauty standards complicate our relationship with our bodies, how the fashion industry perpetuates this and how to stop feeding into it. When it comes to styling, I admit that I used to subscribe to the restrictive fruit-dressing method, where you follow specific styling rules based on whether you're an apple, a pear or whatever. Your figure may be juicy, but it's certainly not edible. Instead of this limiting approach, I will sprinkle science-based tips throughout this chapter to show you different ways to celebrate your clothed body through your style, beliefs and actions.

Body image and the clothed body

You could pick out the most beautiful and expensive outfit in the world. It could be dripping in sentimental value. It could be from your favourite designer in the most luxurious fabric, and even in your favourite colour, and still not feel right. A survey of over 100 women between nineteen and forty years old found that their satisfaction with an outfit depended on how satisfied they were with their bodies.[3] Body satisfaction or dissatisfaction is one of the seven factors that makes up your body image. Body image is the mental representation of your body based on:

1. How you feel about your weight and shape (your body satisfaction or dissatisfaction)
2. How sensory experiences impact your body
3. Your history of weight change or fluctuation
4. Cultural and social norms
5. How you process information, act towards others and think of yourself in relation to others
6. Your mental well-being
7. Your biology and physical health[4]

It doesn't matter if you're a professional fashion model or sit behind a desk all day. Struggling with body-image issues in some form is a universal experience,[5] and your feelings about certain outfits can potentially enhance or impair your body image. Studies show that when an outfit doesn't fit properly, we're more likely to blame ourselves than the clothes.[6] This thought pattern is arguably the most important reason you need to absorb every lesson in this book and rewire your brain to see clothes as the tools they are. This is definitely a case where a good workman *can and should* blame their tools (and get better ones).

Changing rooms

Trying before you buy is an effective way to find the perfect clothes for you. But if this experience is miserable, chances are you won't want to do it often, if at all. I have a love–hate relationship with changing rooms. In the ones with the best lighting, I test the durability of my outfit by perfecting my twerk in the mirror and exit with a silly smile on my face. The bad ones seem to cast a dark cloud over my body that kills my joy and has me rushing to the exit. I'm not alone in feeling like the lousy changing rooms outweigh the good ones, as around eighty per cent of people have admitted to feeling uncomfortable in changing rooms.[7]

Unless you're rich enough to shut down the entire store, you also have to consider the unintentional impact of being around other people when you're out shopping: social comparison. Social comparison can happen in two directions. Upward social comparison is when you compare yourself to someone you perceive as better than you. Downward social comparison is when you compare yourself to someone you think you're doing better than. It's a natural thing to do, and it often happens below our level of conscious awareness.[8] According to studies researching upward social comparison, if you don't feel comfortable with your body image, you're less likely to buy an item, even if you love it, if you see a conventionally attractive salesperson or fellow shopper wearing it.[9] Theodore Roosevelt really snapped when he said, 'Comparison is the thief of joy.'

Ignore the labels

If the sensory experiences and general public are too much to bear, trying on clothes in the privacy of your own home can be an easy solution, but there's still another issue to contend with: size labels.

They take the top spot on the list of things we loathe but can't live without. It's crazy how worked up we get over them, because we can all agree it's silly to be bothered by something that isn't real. And let me tell you, those labels are works of pure fiction.

Vanity sizing is the process of purposely mislabelling garments with smaller-than-accurate sizes to convince consumers that their bodies are smaller. The tactic is particularly effective in societies that adhere to the thin ideal. In such places, smaller size labels have been found to positively impact body image, particularly for younger women.[10] But just because you're a size small in one shop, doesn't mean it'll be the same in another. I'll never forget seeing an Instagram story of a woman laying out four different pairs of jeans. Each pair fit her perfectly, yet they were all different sizes. Starting in the 1930s, consumers began swapping their custom garments for ready-to-wear pieces. This saw the introduction of standardised sizing systems, which aimed to provide consistency and clarity when it came to clothing dimensions. However, most of these sizing charts are based on just two or three body types and do not take into account or celebrate the fact that we're all different.

Many clothing manufacturers are still using these outdated sizing charts, which do not account for increased ethnic diversity, changes in health care and other societal shifts that contribute to the incredibly varied body shapes we see today. In most cases, manufacturers are not adhering to standardised sizing systems at all. Instead, every manufacturer has their own system, and brands use this freedom to give themselves a competitive advantage, which is why we're witnessing the rise of vanity sizing.[11]

Vanity sizing doesn't just make clothes shopping harder; it can send your body image into a tailspin. To detach yourself from the thin ideal, ignore the labels. Look instead for the sizing charts and grab your trusty measuring tape when shopping online. When in-store, go old school and eyeball the garments to see which option would be best to try on. If you can't let go of the labels, try to avoid being hypnotised by the numbers. Instead, question what the outfit is giving and avoid blaming your body for not fitting into a number. If it doesn't fit, remember: there are plenty more 'fits in the sea.

Are you a body terrorist?

'Bodies are not only designators of oppression, but all oppression is enacted on the body.'

Sonya Renee Taylor, The Body is Not an Apology

In *The Body is Not an Apology*, Sonya Renee Taylor discusses our need to eradicate body terrorism from the inside out. She defines body terrorism as 'a systemic and structural issue that underscores how our political, economic and social systems uphold the marginalisation of bodies based on race, gender, age, size, ability, sexual orientation, and various other markers'.[12] We can stop body terrorism by changing our unconscious beliefs about other bodies. Making unwarranted comments about someone's health relative to their size and failing to consider non-able-bodied people are just two examples of how body terrorism is perpetuated in our day-to-day lives. Body terrorism can be extremely harmful, both to others and to ourselves. By only celebrating our bodies when they look a certain way, or by thinking our lives will be destroyed by body changes like weight gain, we're upholding damaging beliefs that only certain bodies deserve to be celebrated. It's essential to change the way we think and talk about other bodies – and our own – because these damaging beliefs are so easily internalised.

Change your self-talk

Don't let anyone tell you you're weird for talking to yourself. Self-talk is an intrinsic part of the human experience. Our internal dialogue helps to shape our beliefs, perceptions and attitudes towards so many things, including our bodies,[13] but it's not always happy days. In my early twenties, the phrase 'I hate my legs' became like a weird religious chant for me. This overtly negative self-talk perpetuated a damaging relationship with my body that spilled into the relationship I had with my clothes. Suddenly, my options were cut in half because I couldn't wear this or that due to the ridiculous hostility I felt towards my legs. I could only break out of this negative loop by incorporating positive affirmations into my self-talk. Positive affirmations are encouraging statements that can help you overcome self-sabotaging thoughts. Repeating phrases like, 'I'm grateful for my legs – they get me where I need to go,' helped me see them in a better light, improved my body image and encouraged me to wear the skirts and shorts I had been coveting but was too afraid to wear.

If positive affirmations aren't really your thing, you may find success implementing the 'don't, not can't' principle. Psychologists Vanessa Patrick and Henrik Hagtvedt discovered that replacing the words 'I can't' with 'I don't' can have a positive effect on goal-directed behaviour.[14] If your goal is to foster a better relationship with your body that benefits your relationship with your wardrobe, then instead of saying: 'I can't wear that because I hate my [insert body part]', replace it with: 'I don't want to showcase that part of my body today, so I will wear something else.' The 'don't, not can't' principle will help you be kinder to your body by focusing on solutions instead of perceived problems.

Fit or flare?

In Chapter 2, I discussed a study that identified clothing fit as a significant factor in how we're perceived. People wearing made-to-order clothing were considered more trustworthy and successful, and thought to generally have a better vibe than those wearing suits off the rack.[15] Another explanation for these findings is that fitted clothes allow us to figuratively take up more space by placing the body front and centre. Showcasing our figures by choosing to wear fitted instead of oversized clothing can be considered an act of celebration. Outfits that enable us to celebrate our figures can instil us with a sense of confidence by saying, 'This is the body I have. Admire it with me.' This confidence can indirectly affect the way we're perceived by others, because when you feel good about yourself, people gravitate towards you.

On the flip side, fitted clothing can have completely the opposite effect. A 2006 study investigated the influence of dance attire on the way female ballerinas perceived their bodies. The results revealed that dancers experienced a significant positive increase in their body image when they wore oversized clothes compared to their tight-fitting leotards, which were partially responsible for increased body concerns.[16] In this instance, fitted clothes were perceived as an invitation for their bodies to be judged. While studies have shown that well-fitted clothing can increase body confidence, it also depends on your body image.[17] For example, research has suggested that when you have a negative body image, you're more likely to choose clothes that cover up your body, while having a positive body image increases the likelihood of you wearing clothes that show it off.[18]

Dressing for your body is incredibly complex. A certain style can be liberating on one body and feel terrifying on another. I've realised that dressing for your body is more about styling yourself in a way that allows you to embody happiness. To me, happiness looks like celebrating the parts of your body you adore while concealing the bits you're not as keen on. This is based on the concept of body neutrality.

Positivity or Neutrality?

The body positivity movement was born on social media to challenge narrow concepts of beauty that traditionally centre on young, thin, white, able bodies. Waves of content featuring marginalised folks who don't fit that mould serve to normalise diverse bodies and show that 'beauty' doesn't just look one way. However, between being co-opted by people who conformed to traditional beauty standards and being commodified by big businesses, today's body positivity movement is not the same grassroots concept we were introduced to.[19] And while it's been proven that body-positive content increases body appreciation among viewers,[20] the road to body positivity doesn't always lead to a positive body image.

The core message behind body positivity is that every body is beautiful, so you should love every part of the one you have. But having a positive body image means acknowledging that bodies don't *need* to be beautiful. You don't have to love every part of it all the time, because, honestly, that can get a little exhausting. Instead, you can accept your body for what it is rather than fixating on how you can turn your negatives into positives.

When you're overly focused on being positive, you can feel like a failure on the days when you're not particularly fond of something you see reflected back in the mirror – but we all have those days, and we don't need that extra pressure.[21] Body neutrality takes the edge off and allows you to make peace with your body as it is. You're in luck, because I have crafted a series of clever styling tips to help you incorporate this revolutionary concept into your daily life.

Here are your best bits

While it's been proven that people tend to use clothes to cover up their perceived flaws,[22] we must remember that what you see as a flaw today might be a cause for celebration tomorrow. This change can be a result of a whole host of things. It can happen as we grow and learn to see ourselves in a different light, or it can happen due to changes in cultural norms. Just think about how old TV shows used to show women fretting over whether or not their ass was fat. Nowadays, the media is all over anyone who has some junk in the trunk. No matter how much we may shun these accepted beauty standards, we can't ignore their impact on the way we see ourselves. You can buy a bunch of clothes that showcase the aspect of your body you like at this very moment. However, you'll save more money by understanding the different ways to style your body to accommodate your changing perceptions.

It's all about the eyes

Shapewear isn't the only way to alter how your body looks. Being selective with your colour choices is a great way to highlight or skim over a specific area of your body. Dull and dark colours in matte fabrics absorb light. The finer features of your body, like curves, rolls or bumps, are absorbed by the density of these shades, which makes your body appear slimmer. (I bet you didn't think there was science behind the belief that black is slimming.) Lighter and brighter colours in shinier fabric have the opposite effect. They reflect light, which makes your features pop, draws attention and makes the general area appear larger.[23] The same effect has also been observed in heavier fabrics like fur.

Gestalt psychology is a school of psychology made up of a series of principles that provide the foundation for the modern study of perception. If we consider some of these principles when dressing, we can ensure that we're emphasising the parts of the body we like and de-emphasising the parts of the body we don't. The Gestalt principle of figure/ground lets the eyes know what it should be focusing on (the figure) and what it should ignore (the background).

Imagine an outfit made up of two colours or patterns, such as a blue dress with a pink floral print around the waist. Our eyes will be drawn to the part of the body with the secondary colour, known as 'the figure' – in this example, that would be the band of pink floral print – while naturally skimming over the parts of the body wearing the primary colour, which is known as 'the background' – in this case, the plain blue parts of the dress. The dress I've just described would be perfect for emphasising the waist, as it utilises the figure/ground principle to break up the dress and draw the eyes to the centre of the body. Similarly, your eyes will be drawn to larger prints, which can be used to emphasise your chosen area, while smaller prints have the opposite effect.

Gestalt's principle of similarity states that when two things appear similar, our eyes group them together. According to this principle, if you were to wear similar prints or colours on the top and bottom halves of your body, they will appear to be proportional to each other.[24] [25]

Moving on from colours, when looking in the mirror, think of the different ways your eye moves across your body when you wear certain shapes. Outfits that include cuts, tailoring or draping that cause the eyes to zig-zag across the body will create the illusion of an hourglass shape, as we see in wrap dresses.

Eye-movement principles get a little trickier when it comes to specific patterns like vertical and horizontal stripes. The idea of vertical stripes being the slimming choice is a myth. In 1925, German physicist Hermann von Helmholtz discovered what is now known as the Helmholtz illusion. He composed an image of two identical squares containing equally spaced stripes – one with vertical stripes and the other horizontal. After several tests, he discovered that the square containing horizontal lines looked taller and narrower than the identical square with vertical lines. The reason for the illusion is that horizontal stripes filled up more space from top to bottom, thus making the square appear taller and thinner than the one with vertical stripes.[26] But squares are no comparison for the human body. Fast-forward ninety-odd years, and studies have observed the Helmholtz illusion in mannequins[27] and humans[28] of all shapes and sizes. Say you're wearing a dress with vertical stripes on a Monday and one with horizontal stripes on a Tuesday. The research states that you'd have to increase your body width by 5.8 per cent on Tuesday for it to look the same as it did the day before.[29]

More than just your average body

> 'A body that does not conform, that transgresses
> such cultural codes, is likely to cause offence and
> outrage and be met with scorn or incredulity.'
>
> *Joanne Entwistle*[30]

Failing to see yourself represented in the media and having a distinct lack of clothing styles available to you damages your self-concept and body image. Seeing something so far removed from yourself being championed as the pinnacle of beauty makes it harder to see yourself as beautiful. There's still a lot of work to be done, but we've come a long way.

Size and shape

> 'Why is size inclusivity in the fashion industry
> important? Because clothes are made to fit
> our bodies, we aren't made to fit the clothes so
> everybody should be able to buy and wear what
> they want to.'
>
> *Jessica Jones, award-winning blogger and
> author of* Own It

Limited clothing size options might seem like nothing more than an inconvenience, but it can have a disastrous effect on the body image of plus-sized people.[31] This kind of marginalisation is easily internalised,

causing people to consider their bodies unworthy. To better understand
the plus-sized market, I spoke to Patricia Luiza Blaj, founder of Loud
Bodies, an ethical, sustainable and inclusive slow-fashion brand featured
in the likes of *Vogue* and *Cosmopolitan*. Patricia explained that brands'
commitment to the thin ideal stems from their desire to sell from the
viewpoint of exclusivity. Their rationale is: 'The more unattainable we
seem, the more we make people think they will never be happy or feel
valuable without consuming our product.' With this tactic, brands may
be trying to kick our FOMO into overdrive, but it's ineffective for two
main reasons.

First, inclusivity is more appealing, and that's just a fact. Studies show
that consumers view size-inclusive brands that work with a diverse range
of plus-size models more favourably than those that don't, which trans-
lates into sales. Secondly, these days more people fit into the plus-sized
category than ever before. A 2020 survey conducted by market research
firm NPD found: '70 per cent of women in the US wear a size 14 (EU 44,
UK 18) or larger. In the UK, the average woman's clothes size is 18, while
EU countries follow a similar pattern.'[32]

Thankfully, data suggests that brands are starting to get their heads
out of the clouds. According to buy-now-pay-later firm Afterpay, the
number of retailers carrying 'plus-size' clothing in the US has increased
by fifty-nine per cent between January 2021 and January 2022. There's
also been a thirty-six per cent year-on-year increase in customers buying
from retailers featured as plus-size.[33] In the UK, the value of the plus-size
clothing market has been rising steadily, and it's estimated to hit around
£9.03 billion by the end of 2022.[34] Size inclusivity doesn't just have a positive impact on body image, it also allows more people the opportunity
to use clothes as a means to fashion their self-identity.[35]

Race, ethnicity and culture

> 'I'm an introvert, but I sometimes feel it's a disservice
> not to wear the brightest colours and be the most
> visible in the room because often, as Black women,
> we're not . . . we're even told not to wear certain
> colours, and so I make sure I wear all of them.'
>
> *Ashley Chew*

Black bodies and the bodies of People of Colour (POC) have long been subject to staunch criticism regarding how we choose to present ourselves. Psychology dictates that POC, mainly Black people, are more saliently aware of their race than Caucasian persons.[36] So, when instances arise where we are under-represented or disregarded (see cultural appropriation page 101), we notice.

For a content series on *Fashion is Psychology*, I spoke to Ashley Chew, an artist, diversity activist and model. We giggled about our shared obsession with colour psychology, and she educated me on what life looks like as a five-foot-eight Black model. 'We're always told we're too much, we're too big, we're too small . . .' These words rang like a hymn from my Catholic school days – dormant yet ever-present. In February 2022, women's basketball coach Sydney Carter went viral after wearing a pair of form-fitting pink trousers. Carter received a wealth of (pathetic) criticism suggesting that her style choices directly and negatively impacted her coaching abilities.[37] What these trolls were really saying is that they're offended by Black women's curves and fetishise any outfit that doesn't drown them.

Like Ashley said, it's always something. It's enraging. When some people get angry, they make statements – I write dissertations. When former *Vogue* editor Alexandra Shulman made the repugnant insinuation that Black models don't sell,[38] my master's thesis empirically proved that to be incorrect.[39] Similarly to plus-size erasure, my paper revealed that under-representation of Black people and POC fosters negative associative reasonings,[40] such as the belief: 'If I'm not represented, then I must not be *that girl*.'

With her creation of the #Blackmodelsmatter movement, Ashley joined the list of trailblazers and activists who demand more from the fashion industry and more for us, to great effect. According to online fashion and beauty news platform *The Fashion Spot*'s diversity report, the representation of Black and POC models has been trending upwards for some time, with the Spring 2022 fashion season currently taking the crown as the most racially diverse season on record.[41]

In 2020, editor-in-chief of *The Cut* magazine Lindsay People Wagner and public relations specialist Sandrine Charles created the 'Black in Fashion Council' to build a new foundation for inclusivity in the fashion industry. In the same year, Aurora James, a creative director, activist, and fashion designer, created the Fifteen Percent Pledge. This US-based non-profit lobbies retailers to pledge at least fifteen per cent of their shelf space to Black-owned businesses. With the rise of designers like Telfar Clemens, Fisayo Longe, Kerby Jean-Raymond and others, POC and Black bodies have been afforded more opportunities to solidify their self-concept and wear their hearts and culture on their sleeves.

Disabled bodies (visible and invisible)

'They think that people need to change to fit in their world, which is why sizing is still so limited throughout the fashion industry. I believe it's our duty as a brand

to create a world that welcomes everybody, and
we as a brand need to change to be able to cater to
more than just one body type's needs.'

Patricia Luiza Blaj

It's hard to consider your clothes as a tool when they aren't functional in
the first place. Patricia's fashion brand Loud Bodies is adaptive and able
to cater to individuals with disabilities, but they're one of the few brands
who do. Between 2019 and 2020, 14.1 million people reported a disability
in the UK, a year-on-year increase of 2.7 million.[42] I'm a chronic pain
sufferer, but I currently don't require the use of mobility aids like some
other folks living with Ehlers-Danlos syndrome. Still, I understand the
challenge of trying to choose clothes that provide support in an aestheti-
cally pleasing way. If any designers feel inspired to make a sexy bodycon
dress that incorporates my bulky back brace, holla at your girl.

'Design thinking' remains one of the most fascinating things I learned
during my fashion psychology degree. It's a problem-solving approach
to design based on human-centred techniques that tackle ill-defined or
unknown problems.[43] For the module, our class split into groups to design
a piece of clothing that was truly inclusive. My group decided to design a
bra that could be used by people who had undergone a mastectomy and
those with physical disabilities. I'll never forget how the room felt when
it dawned on us just how unsuitable clothes are for so many people, an
issue that disability stylist Stephanie Thomas is tackling head-on. In an
interview with *Popsugar*, Stephanie, who works with celebrities such as
actress and model Lauren 'Lolo' Spencer, uses her Disability Fashion
Styling System™ for sourcing and styling. The system includes three pil-
lars: 'Accessibility' (easy to put on and take off); 'Smart for your health'

(medically safe); and 'Fashionable' (loved by the wearer, works for their lifestyle and body type).[44] Providing people with a framework to discover their personal style allows them to be independent, and Stephanie understands how empowering that is: 'I want people to be able to do this for themselves . . . I'm no longer advocating for brands to make adaptive clothing. When brands bring me in now, I am advocating for human-centred universal design.'[45]

For everyone to have a chance to experience Big Dress Energy, the entire industry needs to follow the helm of adaptive fashion brands like I Am Denim, or the likes of Tommy Hilfiger and Adidas, who provide adaptive clothing offerings.

Fashion brands and retailers don't always make it easy for us to improve our relationship with our bodies, but we live in an era where people are not afraid to demand to be seen, heard and catered to. We have twenty-four/seven access to creatives from all kinds of backgrounds, shapes, sizes and abilities, who inspire us to style and celebrate every kind of body. The next step is to take this inspiration, combine it with my tips and give yourself some grace as you work to get your body image to a place you're comfortable with – and keep it there.

Key takeaways

★ When we talk about body image, we should always consider the 'clothed body', because social norms dictate that we spend most of our time in clothes. As the meeting place between our public and private selves, clothes have a significant influence on the way we feel about our bodies.

★ While progress has been made over the years, the fashion industry still needs to address issues such as vanity sizing, inclusivity and representation, both in the media and in retail, to prevent harming the body image of consumers.

★ We can also play an active role in improving our body image by monitoring and adjusting our self-talk, evaluating how we feel about our bodies when wearing particular outfits, and stopping ourselves from wearing things that could cause us harm.

★ Embracing body neutrality can positively impact body image by allowing you to accept your body as it is, rather than pressuring yourself to feel a particular way about it.

★ Dressing for your body is all about using perception and eye-tracking to draw attention to the parts you like and away from the parts you're not so fond of at the moment.

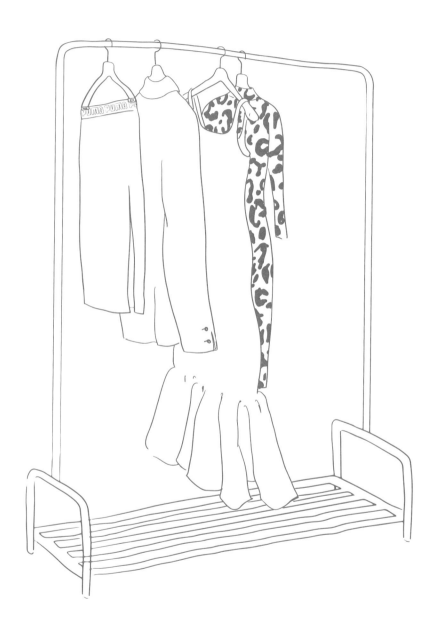

Chapter 7

Hanger management

How to use mindfulness to curate a wardrobe that lasts

'The wardrobe articulates, both spatially and temporally, a set of material and symbolic practices that are fundamental for the constitution of selfhood, identity, and well-being.'

Saulo B. Cwerner, Clothes at Rest: Elements for a Sociology of the Wardrobe[1]

You probably have over 100 pieces of clothing in your wardrobe right now. But let me guess: you still feel like you have nothing to wear. Every time you open your wardrobe, do you let out a little disappointed sigh? Or maybe you've discovered that your 'spring cleaning' clear-out is no longer seasonal – it's happening in summer, winter and autumn, too, because you're not buying pieces that reflect who you are, fit with your lifestyle or make you feel good.

If this sounds at all like you, then it's high time you engaged in some 'hanger management'. I'm not talking about the 'hanger' that turns you into the Hulk when you skip lunch. We're talking about the hangers in your wardrobe.

This chapter will take you through a series of psychology-driven steps that will empower you to transform your wardrobe into one that gives you Big Dress Energy. Before we dive straight in, I have to stress that dressing your best self begins and ends with one of the most important spaces in your home – your wardrobe.

Your wardrobe is like the ultimate music playlist: there are the old-school bangers that take you back to a time when 'life was good', the new-school hits that make you feel alive, the cultural music that makes you feel at home and the alternative songs that speak to your unique tastes. Every piece of clothing you've gathered over the years reveals something about your customs, habits, identities and feelings. Your wardrobe contains pieces that tell stories of who you used to be and clothes that celebrate who you are today. Ultimately, it's the place that connects your past to your present.

Introspection in your wardrobe

'Wardrobe ethnography' is the practice of understanding a person by investigating the contents of their wardrobe. Even the daily process of selecting an outfit from your wardrobe says something about how you attempt to balance your need to express your identity alongside your emotional, functional and aesthetic desires.[2] By simply taking some time to study your wardrobe, you'll be able to unearth important things about yourself and how you've changed over time. There are many different ways to engage in wardrobe ethnography, and it might seem overwhelming at first. Rest assured, below I will reveal six questions that will easily guide you through this reflective process. It's time for you to do some work. So, take out all of your clothes, get a pen and paper, and let's get stuck in.

Question 1: How many items of clothing and footwear do you have, and what percentage of your wardrobe do you wear regularly?

A survey conducted by the North London Waste Authority found that eighty-three per cent of us own at least six items of clothing that we haven't worn in the last year – with some of us admitting to owning 200 unworn items![3] When you go through your clothes and add up everything you own, you might realise you have far too many things.

Look through the contents of your wardrobe and pick out at least three pieces you have never worn or have only worn once or twice. What do they have in common? Ask yourself why you need to hold on to all these clothes you're not even wearing. How often do you shop, and why? How do you feel when you add something new to your wardrobe? Have you grown attached to the feelings associated with novelty? Do you simply have no time to declutter, or have you developed a compulsive shopping habit?

Overconsumption is worrying on a global scale. Across the UK, more than 300,000 tonnes of used clothing go into landfill every year. When we talk about sustainability, we tend to make scathing judgements about people with overflowing wardrobes, but there are lots of reasons why this might be the case, so if this sounds like you, there's no need to feel embarrassed. Perhaps you feel detached from the clothes you buy, or maybe you have too many statement pieces you don't feel comfortable wearing on a day-to-day basis – everyone's circumstances are different. In my experience, we're not going to be able to change our behaviour by chastising ourselves or others. Instead, if you've noticed your wardrobe is bursting at the seams, why not focus on the psychological benefits of a decluttered closet that you're currently missing out on?

According to research, having a minimalist wardrobe and embracing a low-consumption lifestyle can lead to increased life satisfaction, improved personal relationships and general happiness.[4] Think about how relaxed you feel after you tidy your room. Embracing minimalism doesn't just declutter your space, it also declutters your mind. Now you know that all of this and more is waiting for you, are you more willing to make that commitment to a more refined wardrobe?

Question 2: What percentage of your clothing and footwear fits into the following categories?

- workwear
- activewear
- basics and loungewear
- formal wear
- going out-out
- swimwear and beachwear
- outerwear
- accessories

Draw a circle and use your answers to the above to create a pie chart with a segment for each category. When I first tried wardrobe ethnography and answered this question, I realised that my pie chart wasn't aligning with my current lifestyle. I was a bit (read: a lot) of a party girl in my younger years, but now I wasn't going out nearly as much as I used to, and yet about fifty per cent of my wardrobe still belonged to the 'going out-out' category. Why was I holding on to these mini dresses and sequinned cropped tops? I think it's because they reminded me of a less complicated phase of my life, when I had more time, fewer worries and a lot less going on in my mid-section.

However, keeping hold of these pieces meant I had less room in my wardrobe – and my life – for the new Shakaila: her new routine, new body, new priorities and new lifestyle. Once I acknowledged this, I recognised that I was doing myself a disservice. Your clothes can do wonders for you, but only if they are aligned with your lifestyle, and wardrobe ethnography is the first step towards creating that synergy.

The next step is to create a second pie chart to determine the percentage of days you spend wearing clothes from each category in any given month. Then, you simply have to compare the charts to see if they match up. For example, are you wearing activewear only thirty per cent of the time, but it makes up sixty per cent of your wardrobe? Or are you wearing loungewear fifty per cent of the time, and yet it only makes up ten per cent of your wardrobe? Taking the time to answer this question accurately can be a truly eye-opening experience and is a vital step in your hanger management journey.

Question 3: What is the ratio of old to new clothing?

On reflection, do you realise that you have more new clothes than old ones? There are more questions to consider depending on your ratio. Do your clothes last only one to two seasons? Is this due to their quality? Do you fall out of love with them quickly? Perhaps you love to move with the trends – or is the opposite true for you? Do you have lots of old clothes? Are you great at buying clothes that last, or do you have many memories wrapped up in your clothing? Do you find it difficult to part with clothes that remind you of a happier time, or are you simply stuck in a time warp?

More new clothes than old

If you fall into this category, you're not alone. Findings from the Great British Wardrobe Report revealed that seventy-nine per cent of women are happiest or at their most confident when wearing something new, and fifty-two per cent feel lacklustre or less secure when wearing something old.[5]

In a study published in the scientific journal *Neuron*, researchers showed participants a series of images. After participants had become familiar with those images, researchers added a new 'oddball' image. Measurements of participants' brain activity revealed that the brain's pleasure centres lit up when this new 'oddball' image was introduced, resulting in a flood of dopamine – the same feel-good chemical that is released when we eat good food and have great sex.[6]

In another study, conducted at University College London, participants were repeatedly shown a series of cards and asked to draw one at random. Upon turning over their chosen card, participants discovered that some cards indicated a monetary reward. This process of picking a card was then repeated twenty times to allow participants to become extremely familiar with the money-making cards. Through observation, researchers discovered that each time a participant picked the money-making card, the pleasure processors in their brain lit up. Researchers then introduced new cards into the mix. The new cards would either offer a monetary reward or be completely worthless – participants would only find out after selecting the card. You might assume that participants would pick the guaranteed money-making cards over the new wild cards, but surprisingly, the results revealed that participants were more likely to gamble on wild cards. When participants chose these cards, their brain's pleasure processors lit up – regardless of whether or not they'd earned a monetary reward[7] – revealing the power that novelty has over us, and the way we instinctively consider something new to be better. Still, it doesn't mean that you're powerless to protect yourself from novelty's grasp. In the next chapter, when I take you through the process of mindful shopping, you'll learn how to tackle this ingrained desire for novelty head-on.

Aside from our cognitive predisposition, other psychological factors should be considered. Having more new clothes than old ones may also suggest that you're detached from your clothes. Developing a detachment often occurs when your clothes don't make you feel good or when they feel more like a costume than an extension of your true self.

You may also see shopping as a way to try to find yourself through your style. While it's great to use your clothes as a way to lean in to the different sides of your identity, you should avoid trying to construct your sense of self through your clothes. To use a dessert metaphor (because every time is a good time for dessert), you're the cake, and your clothes are the cherry – don't forget that.

Take some time to look through the newest additions to your wardrobe and think about why you bought each item in the first place. This process can set you on the path towards self-discovery. It will bring you closer to figuring out what you actually like, how you like to feel, how you like to be perceived, and, most importantly, what makes you feel good. Buying new clothes without going through these steps first will only confuse you and leave you with a wardrobe perfect for someone else, not you.

More old clothes than new

Having more old clothes than new ones can be a good sign. It can suggest you're buying quality and that you've been successful in finding clothes that reflect who you are and make you feel good about yourself. It could also mean that you're using your clothes as memory banks, so that whenever you slip into an outfit, you feel a rush of nostalgia that boosts your mood.

Every time I wear an outfit that's more than five years old, I feel a sense of satisfaction. These outfits represent my ability to take care of and take pride in my belongings. They speak to a level of self-awareness. These pieces are so *me*, they have survived several fashion cycles and countless new trends. I both literally and figuratively pat myself on the back on these occasions, and have often been known to mutter a coy: 'Well done, Shakaila' – and I'm not ashamed to admit that. My mum tells me to 'Have some behaviour' (her Caribbean way of saying 'Wind your neck in') when she catches me in those self-congratulatory moments, all done up, triumphantly shaking my ass in the mirror, to which I always retort, 'Don't hate'.

If you, too, have managed to buck the societal pressure to board the wear-and-dump train, then instead of feeling lacklustre, you should be celebrating with me. These clothes will go a long way towards helping you understand the styles you feel best in, and they'll also support your future mindful shopping practices. Even if they don't do any of that, they're a great conversation-starter. 'Oh, you like this Puma skirt? Thanks! You know, it's six years old! I last wore it to a Drake concert at the O2. It was a warm September evening . . .'

However, if you hardly ever wear these older clothes you've held on to, this can suggest something worrying at play. Often, people hold on to clothes they haven't worn in years because they want to believe that they might wear them again, despite knowing deep down that this will never be the case. They have this hope because they associate their older clothes with their past selves and past feelings.

> 'Clothing constitutes a material record of a life lived, in places, events, moments and phases – dresses that were worn on special occasions, shoes that were part of a teenage identity, a few baby clothes, even.'
>
> *Nicky Gregson and Vikki Beale, Wardrobe Matter*[8]

As we evolve, we can quickly identify the parts of ourselves we like the most and the memories that played a pivotal role in positively shaping us. During the hanger management process, you'll identify the clothes that hold special significance for you. Like my Puma skirt, these items can help remind you of who you are and support you as you continue to grow. However, if you haven't been wearing these pieces and have no real plans to wear them in the future, it could signify that you're holding on to a version of yourself that should have been left behind long ago: like the necklace my ex bought me that I wouldn't wear, but would occasionally give a dirty look to as I rifled through my jewellery; or the leopard-print catsuit I last wore when I drunkenly fell down the stairs at the Tiger Tiger nightclub in London. These are the kind of things and memories we – I – could do without.

Another reason people keep older clothes they no longer wear is the personal connection they have developed to the bodies that once wore them (a topic we will explore in the next question). Uncovering the strength or weakness of your attachment to your clothes can help you understand a bit more about yourself. These questions should open your eyes to some habits you have formed, both positive and negative.

Question 4: What is the ratio of clothes that currently fit to clothes that do not fit?

The relationship between our clothes and our bodies can get pretty contentious. Some people keep twenty to fifty pieces that do not fit them, and fluctuations in our weight are the leading cause of this.[9] If your wardrobe contains a significant amount of clothes that no longer fit, consider why that is.

Perhaps you've been working hard towards achieving your target weight. If so, then slipping back into an outfit that was once too small or too big can be a gratifying experience. However, you must be aware of how much space these outfits are taking up in your wardrobe. A survey by ClosetMaid, a company that offers indoor storage solutions, found that the average woman considers twenty-one per cent of her wardrobe unwearable, with thirty-three per cent of these unwearable clothes being too tight and twenty-four per cent too loose.[10]

The danger of having a lot of clothes that don't fit is that, as time progresses, it can feel like you're being confronted with failure every time you open your wardrobe. Imagine if every time you opened your front door, someone jumped out and listed all the crap you haven't ticked off your to-do list for the last three years. Rough, right? You may not notice it, but by being faced with these ill-fitting items every day, you're causing yourself psychological discomfort. For some people, this might provide the motivation they need to continue along their weight management journey, but for others (like me), it can get pretty disheartening.

I've been beating you over the head with this, but just in case you haven't realised it yet, I'll tell you again: your clothes should be working for you, and not the other way around. Reflect on why you are keeping things that don't fit you and why your wardrobe doesn't contain clothes that feel right for the current you.

Question 5: Which colours dominate your wardrobe?

Your answers to the 'Embracing your rainbow' chart on page 77 should help inform your response to this question. Create a list of these colours and label it 'Colour list one'.

Is your wardrobe full of colours you enjoy wearing, or do you feel like something is missing? Do you ever wish you had more colours to choose from? By now, you're fully aware of the positive impact wearing different colours can bring. If you're not regularly wearing ones that bring you joy or ones that have positive associations, consider why that is.

The next step is to create a second list ('Colour list two') of the colours you want to wear, and then it's time to put together a third list ('Colour list three'), which will consist of colours you think will work well with the ones you picked out for lists one and two. Now, go back to Chapter 3 to check if the colours in all three lists match up to the image you want to present. If they don't, then it's time to make some edits. For example, do you want to wear lots of reds? Do you remember that shades of red are associated with alertness and arousal? Or do you wear a lot of black? Black, as you know, has been associated with dominance and authority. Aligning your preferences in this way will ensure that you're wearing colours that make you feel good, embody the traits you desire and send out all the right signals.

Wardrobe ethnography doesn't just focus on the individual items in your wardrobe; it also considers the relationship between your clothes. If your wardrobe doesn't even remotely subscribe to a specific colour palette, it will be difficult for you to find cohesive outfits, and this can then contribute to unhealthy shopping habits. Remember, your wardrobe is a reflection of you. If it's not working, this could suggest that you haven't been paying enough attention to how your mood alters when wearing certain colours.

Your next task is to combine all three lists to help you cultivate a strong colour palette. An ideal colour palette should consist of three main sections: core colours, accent colours and neutral colours.

Core colours

Core colours are colours that play the most significant role in your wardrobe. These are colours that feature heavily in the outfits you wear regularly. So, you need to make sure that these colours positively affect your mood, speak to your personality and convey the correct messages.

Your palette should consist of four core colours.

Accent colours

Accent colours don't feature as prominently in your wardrobe as your core colours, so you can have a bit more fun with these. Accent colours are typically a bit more vibrant than core colours, but they should still work well when paired with your core colours to help you create a harmonious wardrobe.

Your palette should consist of three accent colours.

Neutral colours

Neutral colours are the colours that help all the other colours in your wardrobe tie together. They typically consist of blacks, whites, greys and browns, as these colours tend to mix well across various palettes.

Your palette should consist of four neutral colours.

And voilà, now you're the proud owner of a colour palette that is totally *you*. Creating this colour palette doesn't mean you can't wear any other colours again. The purpose of this exercise is simply to make your life easier.

Question 6: How would you describe your top three favourite outfits?

According to some studies, more than seventy per cent of people regret buying certain clothes, and nearly a quarter of people end up returning clothes at least once per month.[11] So far, this hanger management process will have helped you identify the styles you don't like, but it's just as – if not more – important to identify those you *do* like, as this will allow you to build a wardrobe you love. Throughout my career, I've realised that many people don't know what they like outside the social situations and social media algorithms that provide the seal of approval they're looking for. A compliment or a couple of thousand likes on an Instagram post encourages people to think, 'I love this,' despite the fact that most of the time, they've failed to check in with themselves to assess how they truly feel about something when divorced from the opinion of others.

When pulling out your three favourite outfits, think about why they're your favourites. Do you associate them with something positive? Do they make your body look a certain way? Do you feel comfortable when wearing them? Do these outfits make you feel confident? Write everything down and make sure that anything you add to your wardrobe makes you feel this way. Next, acknowledge that you probably should get rid of clothes that don't make you feel even close to the way your favourite outfits do.

> 'If fashion and dress are conceptualised in terms of language and communication, then wardrobes must be seen as the individual vocabularies that underpin that system.
>
> *Saulo B. Cwerner, Clothes at Rest*[12]

Piles as far as the eye can see

In the blink of an eye, life as you know it can change altogether, meaning you need to place extra value on your time and how you spend it. How much time have you wasted searching for clothes in your wardrobe? How often have you discovered a long-forgotten item of clothing that would have saved you a lot of time and energy on one of those 'I have nothing to wear' days? You must take control of your possessions rather than letting them possess you. Ten minutes here and there will eventually start to add up.

Now that you have gone through the process of wardrobe ethnography, you should have an acute insight into which pieces are missing in your wardrobe, as well as the pieces that are no longer serving you and those that will help you navigate life dressed as your most authentic and fulfilled self. Any good wardrobe detox starts with a series of piles, so make some space, remember to lift with your legs and let's get going.

In the first round, separate your clothes into three piles, as follows.

Pile one: Continuing identity

These are clothes that reflect the person you are most of the time (remember this idea from Chapter 1?). They're the pieces you currently wear the most or that you plan on wearing more often in the near future. For example, suppose you have recently transitioned from the corporate world to a creative industry. In that case, you might find you have little use for your sleeveless blazers and are more drawn to your quirky T-shirts that up until now have rarely seen the light of day. When I moved from a large company to a start-up, my outfits definitely changed. (My stress levels also dropped, and my panic attacks went with them, but that's a story for another day and another book.)

Any clothes that go into this 'Continuing identity' pile are keepers, and we'll discuss how to get the most out of them in a little bit.

Pile two: Transitional identity

The pieces in this pile often make the occasional appearance out of your wardrobe, perhaps for specific occasions. These clothes act as a bridge between the person you are most of the time and the person you hope to be. For example, you might realise that you prefer to wear slightly more formal attire, but clothes in your 'Continuing identity' pile consist primarily of comfy basics. Either way, most of the clothes that go into this pile are keepers too.

Pile three: Discontinued identity

The two piles above should not contain:

- anything that no longer fits and hasn't fitted in a long time (see page 140)
- anything that causes an immediate negative reaction (for me, it's a scrunched-up face)
- anything that makes you feel even a little bit uncomfortable, whether physically or psychologically, when wearing it

Any clothes that subscribe to the above belong in this third pile, 'Discontinued identity'. These clothes are the physical embodiment of 'Nah'. The pieces that go into this pile are ones you hardly ever wear because they're no longer fit for purpose or, more importantly, because they reflect your former self. That could be you in a different career, you in a different headspace, you in a foreign country. You're no longer that person – and you're not even *wearing* their clothes anymore. You're just storing them. Last time you checked, did you own a franchise of Big Yellow Self Storage? Honour the person you are today and the person you are growing into by slowly detaching yourself from the clothes representing a discontinued identity. Most, if not all, of the clothes that go into this pile are goners.

Sifting through the chaos

In the second round, you'll determine what to do with all of this organised chaos. The first thing you're going to do is combine the clothes in the 'Continuing identity' pile with those in the 'Transitional identity' pile

Although not everything in the 'Transitional identity' pile is for keeps, we have to combine both piles to help us put outfits together and figure out new combinations that will allow us to refine even further.

Think back to earlier in this process when you answered the two-part question: 'How many items of clothing and footwear do you have, and what percentage of your wardrobe do you wear regularly?' This will have enabled you to identify the clothes you're not wearing regularly. If some of those clothes have made it into this pile, we have more work to do.

After going through this process, your wardrobe and mind should feel a lot clearer. On the other hand, you might be feeling a tad worried about the amount of clothes you're keeping relative to the number of styles you regularly wear. Allow me to suggest a couple of reasons why you may not be making the most of your wardrobe.

Reason one: You haven't figured out how many outfits you actually have

The average person only has five outfits on rotation, which is pretty tragic. People often aspire to be as 'stylish' as others, not realising that they're handcuffing their most stylish selves by failing to explore the breadth of clothes they already own. I get that it can be difficult. Putting together an outfit that you actually like is nothing short of a triumph for some people – and why mess with a good formula, right? But just think about the countless styles you could be missing out on. It's time to kick off another process of discovery. So much self-discovery, so little time.

The easiest (and most entertaining) way of exploring new outfit combinations is by having your own little fashion show akin to the montage moment courtesy of Carrie Bradshaw from the *Sex & the City* movie. It helps to have a Charlotte, Samantha and Miranda to cheer you on, but in the world of iPhones, they're by no means a necessity. Every time you try on an outfit, snap a picture. Start by trying on your top three favourite outfits that you identified in question six. Recalling why these are your favourites will help you as you experiment. Every combination you try on should make you feel close to, if not exactly, how you feel when you wear your favourite outfits. Start with things you've never paired before. Could that top go with that skirt? Those jeans with that shirt and hat? Snap, snap, snap.

Often, the outfits we plan in our heads look like trash in real life, but sometimes they work out, and it's through this process that you can take the number of outfits you own from five to fifty. Companies like Whering and MyDressing have turned digital wardrobes like the one owned by Cher Horowitz in the 1995 movie *Clueless* into a reality. Still, if you can't access these apps, you can conveniently store all those images on your phone in an album titled 'my outfits'.

Reason two: Your clothes are out of reach

I remember one time I watched an entire episode of *Top Gear*. I didn't watch it because I'm by any means into cars. Don't judge me, but I still have trouble distinguishing the BMW and Volkswagen logos. If I was the only eyewitness to a car-related crime, the most the police would get out of me would be, 'It was umm . . . white and, like, a jeep shape.' I watched this entire episode of *Top Gear* because I simply couldn't reach the remote, and a lack of willpower combined with a lot of pizza confined me to an hour of Jeremy Clarkson. Your experience with your wardrobe may not be as terrifying, but a lot of people are wearing the same thing over and over again because they just can't access all of their clothes. If you're in a rush, frustrated, or just plain over it, you're not going to spend the time digging. Getting organised will help you get the most use out of the clothes you love and cherish and stop you from wearing the same five things at eye level.

Four ultimate tips for Hanger Management

There are a tonne of organisation-porn videos on YouTube, so you could really turn this into a whole project if you wanted. Or, if you're a bit lazy (like me), here are four relatively easy tips that can help you get organised today.

Rotate your wardrobe

Being born and raised in London means that words like 'summer' and 'spring' carry little weight. Despite the inevitable truth that you'll be confronted with rain at any point throughout the year, trying to squash your knits alongside your flowy dresses guarantees some of your favourites will get lost in the scrum. As unseasonably cold as it can get here, I've never had to reach for my faux-fur coat between May and September, and I for damn sure don't touch my sandals any time outside of those months. Whether you store your out-of-season clothes in vacuum packs, in a suitcase, in the loft or under your bed, rotating your wardrobe at least twice a year provides easy access to the 'fits that you can use at any given moment.

Store your clothes by category and then organise them by colour

Storing your clothes by category may seem a bit obvious, but it will save you a lot of time if you know precisely where a particular type of clothing lives. Then, why not make your life even easier by organising the clothes within each category by colour. A study investigating visual processing found that we perceive groups of contrasting colours as chaotic and groups of similar colours as harmonious.[13] What's more, the study found that we remember patterns with fewer colours better than patterns with more colours. While this step will undoubtedly make your wardrobe prettier, it also serves a greater purpose in helping you remember all of the clothes you own.

Hang the obvious stuff and stack the thick items

My mum used to own what my sister and I affectionately called 'the jean cupboard'. It was like Topshop had set up a concession stand in our house. The jean cupboard went the same way as Topshop (sad times) and closed down after a little intervention. Save on space by folding things like jeans, hoodies and jumpers. Due to their thick fabric, they can be easily stacked without falling down. I like to keep precious wardrobe real estate for delicate, fancy or structured pieces, and store thick items in a drawer or on a shelf.

Give the direction of your hangers meaning

This is a trick I learned recently, and I was immediately blown away by how simple and effective it is. Once you've taken something out of your wardrobe and worn it, replace it – but change the direction of the hanger.

That way, you can see which pieces you're getting the most out of and which ones you're hardly wearing. So, the next time you go through the process of wardrobe ethnography, answering question one will be a piece of cake.

Mend, repair, repeat

During your montage and while repacking your wardrobe, you may have noticed that some of your clothes need a bit of TLC. A hemline might need lifting, a faded black shirt might be in need of a dye job, or a button may need to be reattached. In *Loved Clothes Last,* Orsola de Castro highlighted how 'repairing something that was designed to be disposable is a statement against quantity vs quality'. As I mentioned earlier, one of the main reasons our wardrobes have become increasingly unmanageable over the years is that people have become detached from their clothes.

One of my goals for this book is to cause a paradigm shift. I want to get people to see their clothes as an extension of themselves. According to a phenomenon known as the 'endowment effect', we place greater value on things we take ownership of. Studies show that the endowment effect also makes it harder for us to part with our belongings.[14] So, just as you take care of yourself by drinking eight glasses of water a day (this is your reminder), exercising and meditating, you should also be taking care of your clothing. Through repairing and customising your clothes, you're fostering a more profound sense of ownership by making them more *you,* which subsequently increases their perceived value.

Simple tips to increase the personal value of your clothes

★ Actually read the care labels – don't just chuck everything into the machine on a thirty-degree wash and hope for the best.
★ Store your clothes with care – don't just haphazardly chuck them into your wardrobe.
★ Explore different types of customisation – don't shy away from the scissors.

Last pile standing

By now, you've probably added a few more bits to the 'Discontinued identity' pile. Clothes in this pile are deemed beyond redemption because they can't be fixed or altered, or because they don't align with your continued or transitional identity. Count the number of clothes in the 'Discontinued identity' pile, and divide that number by two. The number you are left with is the number of *new pieces* you're allowed to add to your wardrobe. It's tough, I know, but being tough will put you on the path to a minimalist lifestyle and will allow you to experience its associated psychological benefits. Following this formula can also prevent you from over-detoxing.

What you do with these clothes next depends on your answer to a couple of questions. More questions, I know.

First, ask yourself if a piece has sentimental value. If the answer is yes find a place to keep it that's not your wardrobe where you can access it from time to time.

If the answer is no, then you have a few options. Sadly, in the UK, more than thirty per cent of our unwanted clothing currently goes to landfills.[15] None of the following options includes you adding to *those* piles.

- You can give your unwanted clothes a new lease of life by trying a spot of DIY. I've been known to deal with tough stains by turning a jumper into a crop top, and I've often turned well-fitting jeans into well-fitting jean shorts. If you don't know where to start, let YouTube tutorials be your guide.
- You can sell your clothes on one of the countless online platforms that make selling them hassle-free.
- You can donate them to your local charity shop.
- You can swap them. While I often used to exchange clothes with my sister and close friends, I wasn't privy to the world of clothes swapping until I worked on a campaign with the North London Waste Authority. According to their 2020 survey, one in five Gen Zs belongs to a virtual swap group.[16] Eleven per cent of respondents said that buying (or swapping) second-hand clothes boosted their mood during difficult times, and eight per cent said that swapping clothes made them feel good about sharing.

Neurological studies have also shown that the reward networks in the brain activate during acts of generous giving. It's called a 'helper's high' and we can experience it even when we benefit from these acts via reciprocity.[17] In short, swapping, selling or donating makes you feel good, so why would you choose to simply throw stuff away?

A new chapter

The desire to chuck things out is alluring because it feels like the start of a new chapter or a clean slate, but detoxing every few months is unsustainable. It means that you haven't committed to the in-depth introspection required during the wardrobe ethnography process. If this sounds like you, remember that being confident in your wardrobe will feel ten times better than any detox ever could.

Right now I'm guessing that you're staring at a wardrobe that's a little on the thin side, but hopefully you've gained a new-found understanding of yourself, what you like, what you dislike and what makes you *you*. Don't think this is the last time you'll ever have to go through this process, mind you. Your wardrobe is as much of a work in progress as you are, and I'm sure you still have a lot more changing to do.

Key takeaways

★ You can gain deeper insight into yourself by engaging in the process of wardrobe ethnography and assessing the clothes you own (whether you wear them or not) to see what they say about you and your lifestyle.

★ Most of the clothes you own can fit into three categories:
  ☆ Continuing identity: clothes that reflect the person you are most of the time
  ☆ Transitional identity: clothes that act as a bridge between the person you are most of the time and the person you hope to be

☆ Discontinued identity: clothes that represent the person you no longer are nor want to be

★ Wardrobe ethnography aims to help rid your wardrobe of clothes in the third category and focus more on clothes belonging to the first two.

★ A cohesive wardrobe can contribute to a more cohesive mindset.

★ Efficient clothing storage and effective care and repair methods are great ways to get more value out of your wardrobe.

Chapter 8

Get in loser, we're going shopping

How to shop smart with science

'I think they should list shopping as a cardiovascular activity. My heart never beats as fast as it does when I see a "reduced by 50 percent" sign.'

Sophie Kinsella, Confessions of a Shopaholic

The concept of shopping sounds so simple. You need something to wear to an upcoming event, or perhaps you want to replace an item that's looking a little worse for wear. So you spend around twenty minutes browsing online or trawling through a bricks-and-mortar shop until you stumble upon your target. You select your size, add it to your bag, check out and go about your business. Ha! If only we were that rational. Alas, we're not.

Each of us is a fantastically messy ball of complicated feelings, impulses and desires, so when it comes to shopping, one plus one rarely equals two.

I would argue that the reason so many of us own enough stuff to fill an entire shipping container is that we don't often realise *why* we're shopping in the first place. Time and time again, psychologists have shown that emotional rather than rational motives drive us to shop. Many moons ago, brand loyalty meant something, but now we're spoilt for choice. When faced with limitless options, we experience a psychological impairment called 'overchoice' that inhibits us from making sound decisions.[1] And if you don't really know why you bought that bag or those shoes or that top in the first place, then they're not going to make much more sense to you once they're added to the heaving pile in your wardrobe. Slowly, these items become audience members in your one-person play, *I Have Nothing to Wear*, which runs seven days a week (rating: zero stars).

This chapter is sponsored by the numbers six and five. You're getting six of the most popular reasons why you shop, and five steps to mindful shopping that will help you make smart, science-backed purchases.

Six reasons why you shop

1. You shop to express yourself

When we shop, we don't just buy clothes, we buy lifestyles. Psychologists have identified a concept called 'product-image congruity',[2] which means that if we come across an item that has 'symbolic meanings that we identify with ourselves . . . we're drawn to it because they act as a form of self-expression'. Brands have caught on to this. Designers are increasingly using their pieces to make a statement. These designs entice us to buy under the illusion that they'll help us to voice who we are and the causes we believe in (like 'taxing the rich' or 'pegging the patriarchy' courtesy of 2021's Met Gala).

2. You would've walked away if it wasn't for those meddling retailers

All retailers possess the same road map – and the final destination on that map is your wallet. To get there, retailers can take two routes of persuasion, which psychologists have labelled the 'central route' and the 'peripheral route'. The central route to persuasion is when you're given every shred of information about what you plan to buy. All of that knowledge is hella persuasive because it makes you feel confident in whatever decision you're about to make. The peripheral route to persuasion is when you're persuaded by nothing more than some external cues and vibes. No important information whatsoever.

For retailers, the central route to persuasion is a lot more treacherous. This route only works if you, the customer, are already motivated to make a purchase. Unless you're provided with concrete facts about an item, facts that will help you make an informed decision about whether or not it's right for you, you're unlikely to make a purchase. As such, retailers face several stumbling blocks when taking this route. That's why it's the route less travelled. The peripheral route is a lot more straightforward, as it's unburdened by the stumbling blocks of facts. Instead, it's smoothed out by superficial external cues, like flattering lighting, soft music, catchy slogans and celebrity spokespeople, all of which stop customers from thinking logically and allow retailers to reach our wallets safely.

Let's look at an example. If you're in the market for a new pair of sunglasses and you go off to compare different pairs based on key information like price, durability and UV-absorption, with the intention of only committing to a purchase once you've found a pair that meets all of your expectations, then you've taken the central route. On the other hand, if you're out shopping with no initial intention of buying a pair of sunglasses, let alone having done any research, yet you still somehow manage to walk out with a pair, then you've been pushed along the peripheral route.

Boy, are retailers well versed in the peripheral route to persuasion. There's a reason why you're more likely to hear soulful house over store speakers than drum and bass. Retailers don't want to create a party vibe that will have you running for the exit and to the nearest bar. Instead, they're more likely to play slow tempo music, which encourages you to slow down and keeps you in the store for longer.[3] The longer you're in the store, the more likely you are to buy something.

Visual merchandising is really just one psychological trick after another. Store layouts are specifically designed to place us in a flow state where we're completely absorbed in the act of shopping and lose track of time. Have you ever wondered why you always get lost in major shopping centres? It's because they want you lost, confused and disorientated, as this strengthens the peripheral route to persuasion – break out the tin-foil hats.

Getting caught up in bright colours and complex layouts is a leading reason why extroverted, sensation-seeking people shop.[4] If you're always on the hunt for new, thrilling adventures, I'm talking about you. On the other hand, introverted people are more likely to be persuaded by highly organised, minimal store environments in muted colour palettes: think TK Maxx versus Uniqlo.

Sadly, you're not even safe from these tactics in the comfort of your own home. Retailers use a tonne of methods, both in-store and online, to persuade you to shop – what psychologist Dr Robert Cialdini famously calls the principles of persuasion.[5]

Principle: Scarcity

'Damn, I have to get those jeans now. They're about to sell out!' Are they *really*? Maybe yes, maybe no, but once you see the magic words 'last chance to buy', panic sets in and stops you from taking a second to think. Next thing you know, you're trying to remember the last three digits on the back of your card. That 'last chance to buy' sign relies on a principle of persuasion called 'scarcity' – or FOMO, as many of us know it.

Principle: Reciprocity

It's 7 a.m. You wake up, bleary-eyed and one year older, to an email from your favourite brand: 'Hey babe! It's your birthday, so here's ten per cent off on us'. You obviously have to get something, right? Not even to treat yourself, but because to not use the code would be plain rude – after all, they went to all that trouble to remember your birthday (yeah, right).

The reciprocity principle is based on the belief that we feel compelled to 'return the favour' and pay people back in kind for what they have given to us. That birthday email and those loyalty rewards are all persuasive tricks that give you an extra push to purchase.

Principle: Consistency

The best example of this principle in action is the 'buy this look' section on a retailer site. It typically appears below the image of the item you're looking at and directs you towards purchasing other pieces that the model is wearing. You might have started out just looking for a skirt, but now the outfit seems incomplete without that top and those tights! Your peripheral route is lighting up like a Christmas tree. At first, this might seem like a helpful way for us to access the genius of the brands' stylists – after all, they're offering their expertise for free! But allowing us to 'buy the look' is an attempt to get us to spend more.

We all have a natural desire to appear consistent because it's comforting. It feeds into our innate desire to show that our decisions follow a logical order. This desire means we're more likely to be persuaded by a decision that aligns with our past behaviour. You bought one piece from this look; you might as well get the others. Research shows that over-thirty-fives are more responsive to the commitment strategy of persuasion and, therefore, take their brand affiliations more seriously.[6] It's probably the reason why mixing logos is still seen as a cardinal sin among millennials while most Gen Zs, according to my assistant, 'Don't care about that lol.' And so we don't just buy an Adidas top, we have to get the leggings and the trainers to match, as if we're all starting for Arsenal FC.

3. You need to prove you're down for the cause

These days, it's not enough to just buy something for the sake of it. With every purchase, you're showcasing your allegiance to something. What you buy and where you buy has the power to say something about what you believe in. Particularly for those who hold strong beliefs about crucial topics like gender equality or the environment, buying something that allows you to showcase your beliefs without you having to do much talking is all too appealing.

4. Because you feel low-key insecure

Admitting that you're insecure can be a bit taboo, but rest assured it's a universal experience and one I'm certainly no stranger to. As we've already learned, clothes have the power to boost your mood, so it makes sense that insecurity can be a leading cause of shopping. To test this idea, psychologists Soo Kim and Derek Rucker essentially made a group of willing participants feel a bit shit about themselves by giving them negative feedback and then watched them shop.[7] (My aunt would have been the perfect candidate for that job. When I saw her for the first time in three years, instead of greeting me with a simple 'Hi,' she thought it would be the perfect moment to comment on how much weight I had gained. Yeah, thanks for that, Aunty. *runs crying to Selfridges.*)

The results of their study revealed that the more insecure you feel, the more likely you are to use shopping as a distraction. Understandably, products that are specifically designed to make you feel better about yourself are particularly appealing. Ever heard of a 'pick-me-up purse'? Even worse, when we're in this state, we'll probably buy clothes 'based on an idealised way we see ourselves, not as we actually are',[8] despite not having taken the necessary steps to become the person we hope to be. I bet the size of that 'discounted identity' pile from your wardrobe ethnography exercise is making a lot more sense now.

5. Because you want to belong

To explain this reason, I'm going to take it all the way back to 1943, when famous American psychologist Abraham Maslow invented the 'hierarchy of needs' in his paper 'A Theory of Human Motivation'. Maslow's hierarchy of needs is an eight-layer pyramid that details all human needs. It starts with our very basic physiological needs, like food, shelter and warmth, and ends with 'transcendence' – at which point you're fully 'actualised' and have achieved your ideal self (if such a person actually exists). Three layers up from the bottom is our 'need to belong'.[9]

As the social beings that we are, we're genetically programmed to align ourselves with others, and we often do this when we buy into the latest trends. When we dress according to what's en vogue, we become part of the cultural zeitgeist, and this gives us a sense of belonging that only encourages us to buy more. Often when we're out shopping, we're doing it to reinforce our social identity[10] – our sense of self based on our group memberships, such as social class, cultural background, or *Real Housewives* franchise allegiance (Potomac all day, baby!). Our need to belong is another reason why social proof – another one of Cialdini's principles of persuasion – has us in a chokehold.

Social proof

Social proof is a general acceptance that the majority always wins. For example, even if you don't initially like an outfit, you're likely to appreciate aspects of it if a lot of people think it's cute. Their approval provides proof (get it?) that the outfit looks good, and our faith in the idea that the 'majority rules' helps to shape our perception. As humans, our desire to connect with and follow one another has evolved to form the bedrock of our community-based society. Social proof is in our DNA, so of course seeing a particular dress with 2,000 likes on Instagram is going to make you picture yourself in it. This concept fits into the 'review' stage of getting dressed that I introduced in Chapter 1.

Relying on the opinion of others to inform our own is a shortcut used to speed up our mental processing during decision-making. Its ability to help us think quickly is another reason social proof is such a persuasive tool. However, the conclusions we draw from social proof aren't always accurate. Who among us hasn't bought a trending outfit that 'everyone' has, only to try it on and realise it simply doesn't work for you? Trusting your own judgement or someone that truly knows you is vital.

6. You just want to feel good, dammit!

Understanding the motivations behind why you're shopping helps you to separate your wants from your needs. But that's not to say we should completely shun our wants, because sometimes giving in to them is just what the doctor ordered.

Comfort shopping, retail therapy or whatever you call it – buying stuff to make yourself feel good – is an age-old concept. Research from coupon company RetailMeNot has found that at least twenty-one per cent of us go shopping to relieve stress, while similar studies have revealed that Gen Z and women overall are the most likely to buy clothes as a pick-me-up.[11] It makes sense that the first generation to have no concept of life before social media would be the more susceptible to instant gratification. But why does shopping give us the feels in the first place?

It's not an exaggeration to say that cutting back on your shopping is chemical warfare! MRI studies on the brain have found that our levels of the feel-good chemical dopamine increase in anticipation of going shopping. So that 'high' feeling isn't even related to the actual thing we're buying, but to the act of shopping itself. Increased dopamine levels are also accompanied by a rush of adrenaline that floods our systems when we enter a new shop and successfully secure something new – oh, and who can forget about that other pesky high, instant gratification.

Shopping is cathartic because it acts as a break from the daily habits that often leave us feeling stressed and exhausted. Let's face it, sometimes life can be downright dull, making it difficult to shake the giddy feeling you get every time you add something to your shopping cart. It's tricky to ignore that buzz because our brains are hardwired to be attracted to novelty. Research into brain health also reveals that bouts of retail therapy are essential to a long and happy life. According to a paper published in the *Journal of Epidemiology and Community Health*, 'Shopping captures several dimensions of personal well-being, health, and security as well as contributing to the community's cohesiveness and economy, and may represent or actually confer increased longevity.'[12]

A study in the *Journal of Global Fashion Marketing* gives us a closer insight into how our mood changes at every stage of the retail therapy experience.[13]

- **Pre-shopping stage:** You generally feel pretty awful, experiencing anything from stress, dejection to anger. The study found that when participants felt like this, they looked to shopping to make them feel better more than fifty per cent of the time.
- **Shopping stage:** Shopping acts as a positive distraction. The participants also reported experiencing 'an elevation in self-esteem, a sense of control, and a social connection'.
- **Post-shopping stage:** All the good feels you experienced during the shopping stage tend to linger, and these feelings can intensify depending on the products you buy. You'll probably feel better if you finally nab a bag you've had your eye on for some time, rather than bringing home a pair of earrings that caught your eye in the moment. In the study, almost all participants reported feeling better and had little to no adverse consequences.

So, can retail therapy really improve your mood? Yes. There is no shame in treating yo' self as a way to deal with life's many stressors. However, the real question you should be asking is: 'Should retail therapy be my go-to response when -ish hits the fan?' The answer to that question is a definitive No.

Although everyone in the study reported feeling better in the post-shopping stage, those feelings were reported *immediately* after shopping. While retail therapy can be a legitimate mood-booster, the therapeutic benefits are often short-lived. With any activities that give you a temporary high, it's best to indulge in them sparingly for fear of getting stuck in a reward-seeking loop and creating negative habits that put you in a worse situation than the one you were trying to heal yourself from in the first place! However, as I mentioned before, this is all way easier said than done.

This is your brain high on clothes

All that dopamine swishing around your body while you're shopping does make you happy, but it can also make you stupid. Studies of the brain have found that dopamine cripples an area of our brain called the dorsolateral prefrontal cortex (DPC), which is responsible for helping us to weigh up pros and cons and generally make good decisions.[14] The temporary damage to our DPC stops us from adequately estimating the value of a product, especially if the price looks good.

Sales are so difficult to resist because all humans are loss-averse. Loss aversion is a concept discovered by psychologists Daniel Kahneman and Amos Tversky in 1979, perfectly explained by the saying 'losses loom larger than gains'.[15] When you're shopping and come across a crazy seventy per cent discount, your need to jump on the seemingly once-in-a-lifetime deal will overpower your judgement of whether you actually want the thing in the first place. When you don't get a chance to think things through, the likelihood of you experiencing buyer's remorse goes all the way up. Buyer's remorse is the mental discomfort that occurs when you make a terrible shopping decision and is more common when you place too much emphasis on the things you're buying to fix major life problems. Clothes are a powerful tool to make you feel confident, empowered and secure, but burying your head in your wardrobe isn't a substitute for making necessary decisions that you know will improve your quality of life.

'My brain made me do it' is sounding more and more like a valid excuse for excessive shopping right about now, but you *will* get laughed out of the room if you try and use it (I'm speaking from experience).

Buyer beware

Retail therapy should be an every-once-in-a-while pick-me-up, like occasionally turning to your pals Ben and Jerry when you feel blue. The keyword here is 'occasionally'. When I hear people say, 'If I just had this, then I'd be happy,' alarm bells start ringing. From that point on, it stops being retail therapy and drifts into what psychologists call 'oniomania' – or 'shopping addiction', in layman's terms. Oniomania affects six per cent of the population in the US and eight to sixteen per cent of the UK population.[16] How can you tell if your retail therapy sessions are veering into oniomania territory? Consider these questions:

- Do you think about shopping all the time?
- Do you often hide your purchases from your loved ones?
- Do you find it difficult to function if you cannot get your regular dose of retail therapy?
- Do you often purchase things you can't afford?

Answering yes to two or more of these questions means it's important to take a step back and re-evaluate your shopping habits. We can't dispute the buzz that comes from shopping, but we must acknowledge how easy it is to get swept away and end up in unhealthy cycles that can reduce our quality of life. So if you want to be a more conscious consumer and embrace minimalism, the first step is to create a reasonable spending plan. With help from Bola Sol, finance coach and author of *How to Save It*,[17] the following spending plan will help you monitor your spending habits and take back some control over your shopping habits.

Bola Sol's tips for smart shopping

There should always be a budget for clothing, accessories and beauty products. What's important to remember is that we don't need to make these purchases every time we get paid. Moreover, if we make quality purchases, we shouldn't need to buy often. Before you buy something new, ask yourself: 'Could I resell it?'

It doesn't matter how long you're planning on keeping something for, it's always good to know if you can make some cash back from it at some point. This question is also a great reminder to keep your items in mint condition.

In addition to these questions, you want to make sure you've got a budget for your wants. There are useful apps, such as Yolt and Money Dashboard, that can help you set a budget and track your spending. Being able to track your spending allows you to check if your budget is realistic or not. Observe your spending habits over a two-month period to see if you're going over budget. If you regularly go over what you planned to spend, it's best to reassess where you're overspending and see if you need to make cutbacks.

As we're on the subject of cutbacks, here are two tips to remember whenever you're shopping.

Tip 1: Use cashback apps/websites

Top Cashback and Quidco are well known in the UK. Sign up for at least one of them and you'll be surprised at the savings you can make at some of your favourite retailers. Also check regularly for discounts online; a Google search never takes too long. Always remember, you shouldn't pay full price just because you can afford to.

Tip 2: Keep the tag and receipt

We all have impulsive moments, and every now and again we might experience buyer's remorse. The best way to tackle this is to keep the tag on and put the receipt somewhere safe. Set yourself a reminder halfway through your refund policy that says, 'Do you still want Item X?'. Try it on a few times and see if it still gives you the feels. If it doesn't, then return it and get your money back. You can choose to put that refund in savings or somewhere else important.

Maths, but make it fashion

Another great way to ensure that you're spending wisely on any new piece that catches your eye is to use a calculation called 'cost per wear' or CPW.

CPW determines the true value of an item by considering the number of times you've worn it and any costs incurred to maintain it. Don't worry. You don't have to be a genius to work this out. It's pretty straightforward:

CPW = Clothing cost + Maintenance costs / No. of times worn

Say, for example, you've bought a really cool dress for £50. Initially, you might think that you've wound up with a bargain, but once you've worn it to a couple of parties and taken your pictures for Instagram, you simply fall out of love with it and donate it to charity. The CPW of that dress is £25. Now, say you bought a pair of boots for £100, and you wear them twice a week for three months before they get scuffed. You then buy revamping scuff cream for £3 and continue to wear the boots twice a week for another month before the seasons change and it's time to whip out the sandals. The CPW for those boots is only £3.22 – and you can still pluck them out of your wardrobe next season! Shopping with CPW in mind will ultimately help you make better choices, and it's part of a larger concept called 'mindful shopping'.

Fashion psychology tip

Do downward-facing dog before going shopping. I know this sounds so random, but a study found that when people experience a heightened sense of physical balance, for example when practising yoga, they're less likely to overspend and are more likely to buy things within their budget.[18]

Get your head in the game

Mindful shopping is to impulse-buying what competency is to Donald Trump. To mindfully shop means that you're fully present in the moment when contemplating making a purchase. You're not buying something on a whim. You're making a conscious decision that takes a host of different factors into consideration, including how you feel in the present moment. Mindful shopping also gives you back a sense of control – and the main difference between shopping as therapy and shopping as an addiction is control. Increased control over your decision-making also engages the central route of persuasion, which not only increases your level of happiness,[19] but will also result in you making better decisions.

Sadly, mindful shopping is no easy feat, especially when we consider all the advancements in technology. While online shopping has undoubtedly made our lives easier, it also makes mindful shopping super tricky. Did you know that, on average, your online shopping basket contains twenty-five per cent more than your basket would when you're at a physical store? And when you visit a store *before* you shop online, the contents increase by a whopping sixty-four per cent.[20]

No matter what we're buying, we all secretly wish that our purchases could come out of someone else's account, and that's because parting with our hard-earned cash causes psychological discomfort. However, consumer and business psychologist Dr Dimitrios Tsivrikos has revealed that people experience less discomfort during digital transactions than physical ones. When you think about it, tapping your phone for a contactless payment definitely feels less 'real' than handing over an actual tenner.

Oh, and don't even get me started on how e-commerce has given birth to the drunk shopping movement. Yes, according to a survey conducted on over 2,000 alcohol-consuming Americans by news outlet *The Hustle*, instead of sexting your ex after one-too-many porn-star martinis like a regular person, seventy-nine per cent of drinkers are now spending around $444 per year drunk-buying clothes and shoes on Amazon. A mess, as highlighted perfectly by the researchers: 'The online shopping experience is already peppered with psychological trickery to make us buy things we don't need. Add in alcohol (which reduces our inhibitory control, self-restraint and decision-making abilities), and you've got a recipe for disaster.'[21]

Five steps to mindful shopping

> 'In the twenty-first century, shopping needs to be based on the decisions of the individual consumer who is informed to prevent them from being seduced by branding experts.'
>
> *Paco Underhill,* Why We Buy

Step 1: Recap on your wardrobe ethnography findings

In the last chapter, you dove headfirst into your wardrobe and made an extensive catalogue of everything you own that fits into your transitional and continued identity. Whether you made this catalogue on your phone with some pics, on a Pinterest board or using an app that allows you to digitise your wardrobe, it's important to refer back to this list before you go shopping. You need to make sure that you're only planning to buy things you don't have (take a look at your pie charts) and things that fit in with what you already own. As highlighted by Paco Underhill: 'The degree to which the modern shopper can inform themselves before the point-of-sale is extraordinary . . . it's a great way to build your rationale.'

These checks will prevent you from creating disharmony in your wardrobe. If you skip this step, things can quickly spiral out of control. Instead of returning something that doesn't fit in with your existing wardrobe, a study found that people get frustrated and simply buy more to go with their new purchase, especially if they've bought something pricey – this is a phenomenon called 'aesthetic incongruity resolution'(AIR).[22] When you're fully aware of what you do and don't own, you'll avoid AIR and make more thoughtful decisions.

Step 2: Pay attention to where you're shopping

Mindful shopping encourages you to be mindful of how you shop and where you shop. People try to be true to their beliefs in every aspect of their lives, including their shopping habits. However, the support for sustainability seems to be growing in conjunction with the popularity of fast fashion. In possibly one of the biggest displays of cognitive dissonance, countless studies have shown that many believe in the former yet buy in to the latter. No one quite has the answers for this, but I believe that stressors in our day-to-day lives weaken our ability to ignore the six reasons we shop I outlined earlier.

It's tricky to manage and it's something that I have struggled with over the years, especially considering how price ranges and size availability can be a barrier to many people trying to buy from sustainable brands. One thing that's important to remember is that sustainability is about more than where you buy from. For example, doing a massive haul and buying a tonne of pieces from a sustainable brand, but then going on to get rid of most of them after wearing them only a handful of times is hardly a sustainable act.

Still, we simply can't ignore the devastating impact that the overconsumption of cheaply made clothing under exploitative practices has on our planet and everyone who inhabits it. While the onus of these practices shouldn't wholly rest on the shoulders of the everyday consumer, the following tips are a good entry point for anyone who wants to achieve more balance between their beliefs and their behaviour.

- Shop second-hand first
- Swap don't shop
- Try made-to-order

I know I've already mentioned the first two, but they're always important to keep in mind. And what about made-to-order items? When you shop from made-to-order brands, you can rest easy knowing that they're making just enough to fulfil demand, resulting in a production process with minimal waste. Buying from these brands also ensures that you're not making impulse purchases, as you know that a unique piece will take a while to arrive. Waiting five months for my Telfar bag was a truly humbling experience, but I had a little joy in my heart every day knowing that something good was being lovingly made and making its way to me. The same is true for three pairs of trousers I'm having to wait two months for from Amazon's The Drop range. While these pieces are typically more expensive than off-the-rack items, the CPW makes it worth it.

Step 3: The four, three, two, one rule

If you've tried the options above but still can't find what you're looking for so need to shop at more mainstream brands, then you can rely on this mindfulness practice to help you buy less and buy better.

Four years

Before you buy something, ask yourself if you will still be wearing it in four years' time. Mindless shopping purchases often tend to be fad items with no longevity that will find themselves in your 'Discontinued identity' pile sooner or later. Avoid this wastefulness by picturing your future self in the outfit. If that image doesn't look right, walk away.

Three outfits or occasions

If you can envisage yourself wearing the thing you're planning on buying on at least three different occasions or with three different outfits, that's a sure-fire way to tell if an item has longevity.

Two deep breaths

In through the nose and out through the mouth. All of that dopamine and adrenaline flooding your system before shopping makes you lose focus, and mindful shopping is all about being present. Taking a couple of deep breaths tells your sympathetic nervous system to calm down.[23] The result? Less anxiety and increased concentration.

One night's sleep

Put the laptop down, put the hanger back on the rail and lay your head down on that pillow. It's the same rule I have when I'm about to send an essay-long text to someone who has royally pissed me off. After a good night's sleep, that text looks very ridiculous – and the same might go for the coat you're planning to buy. If you wake up and still can't stop thinking about it, that should be a sign that you're making the right purchase.

Step 4: Make the most of your community

In *Why We Buy*, Paco Underhill asserts that 'the average time spent in a dressing room has gone up because people use FaceTime and social media platforms to connect with their friends and get their opinion on what they're trying on'. He suggests that relying on a trusted peer who has your best interests at heart is like having your own personal shopping assistant. What you choose to buy is a decision you shouldn't take lightly, and, as with any critical decision, two heads are better than one.[24]

Step 5: Check yourself before you wreck your debit card

Being a mindful shopper means that you have to check in with yourself and how you're feeling before you shop. As I mentioned earlier, feeling powerless and insecure is one of the leading causes of shopping, but feeling larger-than-life can also have the same effect. Studies have shown that when people feel prideful, they're drawn to buy stuff to help them show off; expensive things like luxury watches, shoes and going out-out clothes.[25] Instead of shopping when you feel super high or super low, I encourage you to do a mental audit and only touch your debit card when you're feeling reasonably content.

Key takeaways

★ Social proof, needing to belong, FOMO, self-expression, the desire to increase your mood and the persuasive tactics of retailers are the six main reasons we shop.

★ Retailers use several psychological tricks to push us down the peripheral route to persuasion that causes us to become swept up in the dopamine and adrenaline rush of shopping and make rash decisions.

★ One of the main reasons we keep buying new clothes is because our brains are predisposed to be attracted to novelty.

★ Before buying something, conduct a cost-per-wear analysis to prevent you from buying things you will get little use from.

★ Practising mindful shopping is the best way to counteract the psychological rush of shopping, and you can do this by:
   ☆ recapping on your wardrobe ethnography findings
   ☆ being mindful of where you shop
   ☆ enacting the four, three, two one rule
   ☆ relying on your community for advice
   ☆ only shopping when you feel emotionally stable

Chapter 9

Beauty psychology

Skin, make-up, hair and the mind–body connection

Clothes act as a second skin, but they're no substitute for the skin you're in. Your cosmetic choices, such as the way you style your hair or wear your make-up, are often considered to be inextricably linked to your identity. In some situations or cultures that place limitations on the way you dress, your cosmetic choices can be the only opportunity to express your authentic self and show some individuality. This knowledge, plus the fact that I'm equally obsessed with all things hair and beauty, meant I couldn't possibly pass up the opportunity to delve into this richly researched area.

You can easily take off an outfit that's not working for you and slip into one that gives you more Big Dress Energy, but there's more of a process involved when it comes to your skin and hair. This process can take anywhere from ten minutes to ten months – or it can be never-ending. It's easy to think of facials, haircuts and make-up as a superficial climb towards a specific image or ideal, and sadly, sometimes that's true. We can't deny some of our everyday decisions, from the way we contour our noses to the way we style our hair, are influenced by ever-changing and often restrictive beauty standards. A random decision will be made every few years, like 'thick eyebrows are in, thin ones are out', and over time, we'll cancel our bi-monthly threading appointment and start googling 'microblading near me'.

When you plunge headfirst into this side of the beauty world, it's easy to see it as a place with no room for individuality, but that's not always the case. A 2014 study proved that 'what's good is beautiful', by revealing that people judge those with good personalities as more physically attractive.[1] As much as we're influenced by external opinions, we possess the power to resist conventions and cultivate our own perceptions of beauty. You probably rolled your eyes whenever you heard the phrase 'beauty is in the eye of the beholder' as a child, but now you know it wasn't just a lie from adults seeking to soothe your coming-of-age insecurities. It's scientifically proven. What many people don't know, however, is that beauty is also in the *mind* of the beholder.

In this chapter, you'll discover the little-known field of psychodermatology, which explores the role your mental well-being plays in shaping your appearance for better or worse. I'll also explore how your skincare, haircare and make-up routines do more than just make you look good. I get why people distrust these daily practices being touted as 'self-care'. Cheeky marketing executives like to use the self-care angle to sell you more stuff, and some of the messaging can be overstated. Your problems are unlikely to melt away after switching to a new toner or going for a big chop, after all. But having said that, we should never underestimate the value skin, make-up and hair routines can bring.

Think yourself beautiful

'Think yourself beautiful' might sound like a headline on an early-2000s magazine cover, but I'm not talking about beauty in the traditional sense. I'm talking about the scientific concept that our minds can physically alter how we look. Think back to a time in your life when things were going well. Perhaps you'd just been offered a new job, set off on holiday or fallen in love. Do you remember people commenting on how you were 'glowing'? (Although they probably didn't need to tell you this, because you own a mirror and saw what you were working with.) I bet you didn't change a single thing about your routine, but damn, did you look good! Now, think about a time in your life when you took a loss: when everything seemed to be going wrong, and even though you were getting sleep – sometimes too much sleep – people told you that you looked tired (which we all know is code for 'like crap'). This phenomenon is one example of the mind–body connection.

The mind–body connection explores how every mental state has an associated physiological response that impacts our overall health.[2] It can be something as simple as having a runny tummy when nervous, or more severe issues, like high blood pressure resulting from stress.[3] Stomach ulcers, back pain, fatigue and so much more have been linked to stress stemming from significant life events, both good and bad. If you're having trouble thinking about a good type of stress, try being a bridesmaid. You know you're working towards something great, but jeez, if you could only get there a little faster. Life's stresses wreak havoc on our bodies, and because our mental states can be both conscious and unconscious, we often don't realise why our bodies react or feel the way they do.[4] Sometimes it only clicks that something's wrong when we see the visible effects of stress in the mirror. When psychiatrists and dermatologists noticed this, they joined forces in the early 1800s, and psychodermatology was born.[5]

The skin is our largest organ. It helps us regulate our body temperature, allows us to feel pain and pleasure, and produces hormones like vitamin D, which supports teeth, muscle and bone health.[6] Psychodermatology essentially explores the mind–body connection as it relates to the skin across three areas:

- skin problems that are created by emotional states
- psychological issues that occur as a result of skin problems
- psychiatric problems that manifest themselves via the skin

In an effort to prevent this chapter from turning into a textbook, we'll only explore the first two areas in detail.

How you feel changes how you look

'You've heard the phrases "good skin day" and "bad skin day" – those three little words that can put a pep in your step or trample your self-esteem, because for many of us, how we feel about our skin impacts our quality of life.'

Dija Ayodele, Black Skin[7]

Happiness isn't just good for the soul – it's the difference between looking good and looking great. Studies have shown that feeling happy promotes the release of a chemical called oxytocin that slows down the process of skin-cell ageing[8] and keeps you looking fresh-faced. If we could all maintain a constant state of happiness, the Botox industry would combust. Unfortunately, life doesn't work that way. We're constantly facing bad news, bills and bloody pandemics, which all serve to temporarily swap our joy for stress.

Stress is your skin's arch enemy. Our skin houses immune cells that protect us from infections and aid in tissue reconstruction, among its many jobs.[9] When we're stressed, the brain and nervous system team up to sound the alarm to the skin's immune cells. When this happens, stress hormones like cortisol and adrenaline are released, triggering or exacerbating a host of skin problems such as slow repair, accelerated ageing and acne.[10]

Slow repair

As a self-confessed clutz, I'm no stranger to the occasional scrape or cut. So far this year, I've repeatedly dropped my phone on my face, twisted my ankle while walking down the stairs and sliced open my finger while cutting an apple – and it's only February. Hopefully, you're not quite as accident-prone as I am, but we all have the same expectations of our skin. Discounting severe incidents, we rely on our skin to heal naturally. We trust it will do what's necessary to restore itself to its former glory, and we resist the urge to pick at the scabs we know are on their way. Unfortunately, though, your skin has trouble working correctly when your mind isn't right. When you're stressed, the hormones your body releases dry out your skin, which negatively impacts its barrier function and prevents it from repairing itself.[11]

A 2001 study investigated the factors that affect skin repair by getting volunteers to participate in a low-grade waxing exercise where they had to repeatedly attach sticky tape to their forearms and then strip it off. Ouch, am I right? The researchers discovered that volunteers healed significantly faster when their stress levels were low compared to when they experienced periods of high stress.[12]

Accelerated ageing

Stress hormones break down our skin's collagen and elastin, resulting in inflammation, the development of lines and wrinkles and accelerated ageing.[13] Experts such as Dr Sheena Vaughan, a registered Chinese medicine practitioner, have managed to link certain signs of ageing with specific mind states:

- Forehead lines: worry, shock and anxiety
- Crow's feet: frustration, tension, decision-making
- Jaw tension: resentment, anger or unexpressed emotions
- Frown lines: frustration, impatience, suffering or concentration
- Lines under the eyes: grief, sadness, lost love or stress
- Nose lines: sadness or anger [14]

Studies have shown that lines and wrinkles can interfere with our ability to express emotions. As we age, some of these lines become permanent. Even when we're feeling OK, these lines can be mistakenly attributed to negative emotions, causing us to feel misunderstood and eventually leading to more stress.[15] Feeling misunderstood is no fun, but it's certainly not the main driver behind the wealth of anti-wrinkle products and the rapidly growing anti-ageing market.

The anti-ageing market is expected to grow by thirty-two per cent between 2022 and 2026, at which point it'll reach an estimated value of $88.3 billion USD.[16] Our youth-obsessed media makes ageing seem like a crime. I used to think of life as a series of carefully orchestrated moves leading up to the ripe old age of thirty, after which it would all go downhill. Idiot! My experience of grief made me realise that ageing is a blessing, one that many people aren't fortunate enough to experience. We all need to accept that our looks will change as we grow. Our boobs will sag, and our once sharp jaw lines will soften. It's just a shame that these changes don't always happen naturally. Research from the cosmetic clinic Uvence discovered that over 6 million Brits believed that stress stemming from the Covid-19 global pandemic caused them to age by up to five years.[17] It's a hard pill to swallow, but our skin's internal clock presses fast-forward when we're feeling low.

Beauty psychology tip

Stress wreaks havoc on your skin, but luckily there are some simple tips that can help you nip it in the bud.

- **Shake it out of your system:** Being active has been proven to reduce the emotional intensity of stress by pumping you full of endorphins, another type of feel-good neurotransmitter.[18]
- **Connect with others:** I know when I'm stressed, the first thing I want to do is shut out the world – but that does more harm than good. Research has shown that sharing your problems with other people prevents you from seeking out negative coping mechanisms and helps you cope better with stress. Older people with larger social networks have also been found to have better cognitive functions.[19]

- **Stay present:** Stress often occurs when we catastrophise the future or ruminate on the past. Mindfulness exercises encourage you to stay grounded by focusing on the present moment, and this has been found to reduce stress.[20]
- **Pay it forward:** Professor Cary Cooper, an occupational health expert at the University of Lancaster, suggests that the helper's high that comes from altruistic activities like volunteering makes people more resilient to the effects of stress.[21]
- **Unwind:** Never underestimate the power of relaxation. Studies have shown that whatever form it takes, whether it's a hot bubble bath or a chill night in, relaxation not only reduces stress but also improves concentration, lowers blood pressure, improves sleep and more.[22]

Acne

Pimples, whiteheads, blackheads ... Whatever form it comes in, we can all agree that acne sucks. It's one of the most common skin conditions, affecting most people at some point in their lives, most notably during adolescence. Acne can occur due to diet, facial products or ineffective skincare routines, but people often forget that stress can also give us acne. Stress hormones reduce our blood flow by constricting our capillaries, veins and blood vessels, and increasing perspiration. Additionally, they cause the skin to overproduce oil, which clogs your pores and also dries out your skin by tricking it into thinking it's hydrated when it's actually quite parched. These factors cause tiny sacs of dead skin, natural oils, bacteria and white blood cells to form under the skin, and dreaded acne is born.[23] We aren't always aware of the way stress messes with our skin. Our mindset can cause us to exacerbate or even create skin problems that didn't previously exist. If given a chance, we would reach into ourselves, transform into one of those pompous nightclub doormen and tell those pesky stress hormones, 'Not tonight, lads.' Alas, it's out of our hands . . . until it isn't.

I have a confession to make. I'm one of those people who watches pimple-popping videos on YouTube. I'm a fan of Dr Sandra Lee, aka Dr Pimple Popper. Despite missing a lot of the action because I can only watch through my fingers, I can't seem to ignore the siren song of an unsqueezed lump. Watching a pimple form on my own skin without touching it is an exercise in self-restraint – but when you're sad, stressed or lonely, there's no such thing as self-restraint, only impulse. My fellow pimple-poppers and I aren't in denial. We're fully aware that those anti-acne products have no chance of working unless we leave our damn skin alone. Popping pimples results in inflammation, scarring, hyperpigmentation and the spread of bacteria, which leads to what? More pimples. OK, so if we know this, why do we keep doing it?

In extreme cases, pimple-popping and skin-picking can signify an obsessive-compulsive disorder that affects roughly one in twenty people.[24] As for the rest of us, a brilliant article in *Vice* perfectly outlined why we can't stop the pop. First, popping pimples creates a 'cathartic rush of satisfaction' accompanied by our good friend dopamine. Low moods arise when we lose control, and if you're a bit of a control freak (guilty), then successfully eradicating your face's little invader with your own two hands can make you feel like you're getting some of your power back.[25] That's when pimple-popping stops being about improving your appearance and becomes a self-soothing practice. When you're trying to resist the urge to pop a pimple, try vicariously popping by watching a video instead. It can be almost as soothing. It's gross, I know, but this is a judgement-free zone!

Beauty psychology tip

When you don't have any acne spot treatments, your resilience is low, and you see a random pimple, try to pop it safely. Make sure you have clean skin and hands, a sterile pin or needle, a cotton pad to wipe up the pus and antibacterial ointment to heal the affected area.[26]

And to think, this is just the tip of the iceberg. The mind–body connection impacts under-eye bags, hyperpigmentation, hair colour (studies have proven that stress can temporarily turn your hair grey![27]) and more.

Our mindset can affect our appearance without us lifting a finger, but when it comes to the damaging habits we pick up to manage stress, we can explore techniques to help us break the cycle – like, in this example, popping spots when we're stressed and that stress leading to more spots and the presence of more spots making us stressed. You can go old school and snap a rubber band on your wrist every time you get the urge to engage in an unhealthy skin practice to create a negative association, or you can get all techy and download an app that tracks your milestones and rewards you for reaching them – (so far I've made it three weeks without popping, yay me!) In the meantime, we still have to deal with feelings of disappointment when our external appearance falls short of our standards.

How you look changes how you feel

Psychodermatologists also work to legitimise the impact of skin conditions on our mental well-being. Some people are incredibly insensitive when it comes to skin. They'll tell you 'it's not that bad', that you should simply cover it up and ignore it, not realising that it can have a huge impact on your quality of life.

According to a 2002 study by dermatologists Benjamin Barankin and Joel DeKoven, skin conditions 'can produce anxiety, depression and other psychological problems that affect patients' lives in ways comparable to arthritis or other disabling illnesses'.[28] For example, rosacea is a long-term skin condition that causes: 'blushing or flushing and visible blood vessels in your face. It may also produce small, pus-filled bumps.'[29] In 2014, the National Rosacea Society conducted a survey on over 1,000 rosacea patients. More than half of the respondents claimed to avoid face-to-face contact, and forty-three per cent experienced depression. A staggering ninety per cent reported having low self-esteem and low self-confidence.[30] Acne, in particular, has been found to cause significant emotional problems, negatively impacting self-esteem and self-image while fostering feelings of social isolation and hindering relationship development.[31]

Before diving into professionally advised treatment plans, people with skin conditions should be given the space to actively voice how their skin affects them.

Skincare is self-care

People typically feel energised by their morning skincare routines and relaxed by their night-time ones, but you're actually fostering a sense of calm on both occasions.[32] Any skincare routine will activate your sense of touch, whether you're cleansing, exfoliating or moisturising. Manipulating your skin in this way doubles as a form of massage that stimulates your somatosensory cortex, a region of the brain involved in processing sensory information, and the insular cortex, the area of the brain that processes emotions.[33] Accessing these areas via your daily skincare practices decreases your level of stress hormones and increases dopamine and serotonin, leaving you feeling relieved[34] and birthing a positive feedback loop. The less stressed you are, the more favourable your mental well-being, which positively affects your skin and increases the effectiveness of your skincare products. And – you guessed it – this, in turn, makes you happy. By investing in yourself and carving out a portion of the day to complete a skincare routine, you're actively engaging in a valid form of self-care.

The harsh realities of modern living constantly threaten to interfere with this positive loop, so it's essential to develop a robust routine that you can stick to.

The stuff that's missing from your skincare routine

We're often bombarded with updates on the latest skincare technologies and advancements, so when it comes to finding a routine to support our specific problem or skin type, we're spoilt for choice. Annoyingly, many of these routines fail to acknowledge the mind–body connection, which means they cap the effectiveness of every action you take because your mental well-being has the power to fight whatever acid or serum you put on. To help you enjoy more good skin days, I've partnered with Alicia Lartey, a UK-based aesthetician, to create 'The Beauty Psychology Routine' below.

Everyone has to consider their individual skincare needs when trying a new skincare routine, but the great thing about this five-step routine is that it isn't rigid. It includes transferable skincare philosophies to allow you to seamlessly incorporate psychodermatology into your daily life.

Before we dive into the five steps, I'm going to take you through three techniques you need to use throughout the routine in order to achieve maximum effectiveness:

Technique 1: Use the palm of your hand

Using the palm of your hand to apply your products will help you to reduce product waste (a zero-waste alternative to cotton pads) and cover a wider surface area, but there are also psychological benefits. Research by Japanese cosmetic company Kao has shown that the tactile stimulation of the palm to the face during your skincare routine can increase the level of oxytocin present in your saliva.[35,36] Commonly known as the love drug, oxytocin is a hormone that has been linked to warm, fuzzy feelings, as well as a reduction in stress and anxiety.[37] By reducing your stress levels, lowering your heart rate and just generally making you feel good, this technique has been found to lead to an improvement in skin appearance.

Apply this technique whenever you see the (p) symbol.

Technique 2: Mini-meditations

When life gets busy, we tend to rush through everything, including our skincare. Taking a moment to revel in this everyday routine can do wonders for your skin. Research shows that engaging in mindfulness activities, like meditation, reduces stress and anxiety and improves the overall condition of your skin. For example, psoriasis patients are often advised to treat their condition with phototherapy (an artificial light treatment). One study found that patients who combined phototherapy with meditation needed forty per cent less light exposure than patients who did phototherapy exclusively.[38]

For a mini-meditation:

- Close your eyes.
- Take a slow and deep inhale from your belly as you count to five.
- Imagine each of your body parts filling up with air as you inhale.
- Once you reach five, reverse this process and exhale for five.
- Your belly should contract as you exhale. Imagine your body constricting.
- While completing this exercise, visualise tension releasing from each body part.

Apply this technique whenever you see the (m) symbol.

Technique 3: Visualisation

Visualisation is a powerful technique to improve your skin's condition. Harvard psychologist Ted Grossbart, who specialises in psychoderma-tology, found that when patients focused 'on an image associated with the desired change, whether it's warmer, cooler, dryer, moister or less itchy skin' they experienced a marked improvement in their skin.[39] So, for example, if you have dry skin, you may visualise a moisture-rich environment, whereas someone with oily skin may visualise a cool, dry environment.

Apply this technique during or after a step whenever you see the (v) symbol.

The beauty psychology routine

Each step can take anything from 30 seconds to 1 minute

Step 1: Cleanse *(p, m)*

This fundamental part of the skincare routine can be broken down into two steps. The first cleansing step is ideal for removing sunscreen and make-up. A first cleanse usually involves a cleansing oil or balm, micellar water or a cleansing wipe. The use of a cleansing oil or cleansing balm is preferred, as this allows for minimal friction and effort to remove make-up. Cleansing balms can be used with a muslin cloth, which is suitable for most skin types (excluding sensitive skin and those with inflamed acne). The second step of cleansing can be with either water or a cleanser of your choice that suits your skin type.

When cleansing the skin, Alicia advises using a cleanser for no more than thirty seconds. However, if your cleanser includes active ingredients, such as salicylic acid and benzoyl peroxide, you may want to leave it on for one to two minutes to allow it to work – this is a technique known as short-contact therapy. In clients with eczema or atopic dermatitis, you can use a cleanser with goat's milk instead. Cleanser can also be massaged into the skin using movements linked with lymphatic drainage to increase oxytocin in the body. Lymphatic draining is the practice of performing massage movements towards your nearest lymph node, to aid circulation.

Step 2: Tone

This is one of the most popular skincare steps, and a broad range of products fall into this category. The technique of toning usually refers to applying a product after cleansing. There are hydrating toners, astringent toners and exfoliating toners; the type of toner dictates the process and frequency of application. Using a solution containing exfoliating acids, such as glycolic and salicylic acid, requires precise application, usually using a cotton pad or the fingertips. Exfoliating toners should not be used in conjunction with other exfoliating treatments or certain prescribed treatments. Unlike an exfoliating toner, hydrating toners containing ingredients such as polyhydroxy acids, glycerine and hyaluronic acid can be applied less precisely using the palms of the hands in a cupping motion.

Step 3: Apply treatment *(v)*

The treatment portion of a skincare routine typically encompasses active ingredients that can either be obtained over the counter (without prescription) or from a prescriber. These active ingredients and their use, as well as concentration, are dictated by the MHRA (UK) and FDA (US). Treatments containing azelaic acid at strengths of zero to fifteen per cent can be obtained without a prescription; however, a prescription must be obtained for access to a twenty per cent azelaic formulation. Azelaic acid can be used to treat a number of conditions, including but not limited to acne vulgaris, atopic dermatitis and melasma. It is advised that any treatment used is applied as instructed on the bottle. Positive visualisation can be introduced at this step of the routine in order to increase the effectiveness of treatment.[40]

Step 4: Moisturise *(p, v)*

As moisturising is often considered the most sensual step of the skincare routine, Alicia agrees it's the perfect time to practise visualisation, while also reflecting on the positive parts of your skin and your entire being. Using the palms of your hands to apply moisturiser will also allow you to warm up the product, improving the sensory experience. If a skincare routine is performed in the evening, this is usually the last step of the routine.

Step 5: Apply SPF *(p, m)*

Sunscreen should always be applied as instructed on the packaging, and should always be the last step of your morning routine. Ending your routine with a mini-meditation break is a great way to start the day in a more mindful way.

Face = beat to the gods, Hunny

Unlike the rest of your body, your face is one area where it's not risqué to be bare, and many prefer it this way. If you've tried the tutorials, bought the brushes, and concluded that make-up is not your thing, that's more than OK. I'm not one to cajole people into wearing something that doesn't feel right for them, so if make-up isn't for you, feel free to skip over this next section and we can get to discussing hair.

For the make-up lovers, let's get into the power of a beat face.

Many studies have explored the positive impact of make-up on external perceptions. Make-up wearers are generally seen as more attractive, more sociable and even healthier,[41] but I'm choosing to gloss over this research because, quite frankly, it's pretty well known. Increasing your physical attraction may be one motivation behind wearing make-up, but it's certainly not the be-all and end-all. Avoiding singlehood has always been front and centre in classic cosmetic studies, but recent research has discovered that this reason is over-emphasised.[42] The cosmetics industry is projected to hit $758 billion USD by 2025.[43] It's improbable that most of that is being spent in the name of love. Like skincare, applying make-up positively impacts the mind–body connection by stimulating three senses: touch, smell and sight, and 'the positive stimulation of these senses by make-up can induce sensory and psychological pleasure'.[44] If someone's make-up look isn't to your taste, that's fine, but remember that one person's 'overly exaggerated eyeliner' is another person's form of self-care.

In their 2020 paper, 'Paint a Better Mood? Effects of Make-up Use on YouTube Beauty Influencers', self-esteem researchers Alison Tran, Robert Rosales and Lynn Copes interviewed nine Black, Hispanic and white UK and US beauty influencers aged between twenty-one and forty, and uncovered different motivations behind our love of make-up.

Four reasons why we love make-up that have nothing to do with trying to meet our soulmates

1. It helps us explore our identities

The time you take to beat your face can become a moment of self-reflection when you create a make-up look that allows you to become 'keenly aware of who you are'.[45] In their study, Alison Tran and her colleagues discovered that 'make-up practices are part of identity formation, since using cosmetic products brings the interior self to the exterior'.[46] If I wake up feeling daring, I can use a bold lip colour to help show that, while I might lean in to a soft glam look if I feel delicate. Make-up doesn't create self-worth, but it helps bring our inner worth and feelings to the body's surface, thus helping us create a more 'authentic self'.[47]

2. It's fun

Make-up is fun because it puts us in a good mood by eliminating or reducing feelings of worry and guilt.[48] It's also fun because it allows us to be creative. I may not have an easel, but I definitely feel like a world-class artist when creating an intricate eyeshadow look. Arguably, we all used to be a lot more creative with our make-up looks back in the day. Before social media, you didn't have any tutorials to follow. You had to go to Superdrug or Boots and then figure it out. The results weren't always excellent, but it was certainly interesting. As much as you can be inspired by tutorials and learn new techniques (I know I do), try to avoid being overly reliant on them. Fostering your own make-up style will enable you to express your unique point of view, which will ultimately be more fun.

3. It helps us to navigate the day

Make-up wearers often feel energised after their morning application. This process can help you prepare for the day by cultivating a version of yourself best suited for the situation you're heading into, and that doesn't stop in the morning. Throughout the day, you can make tweaks and changes to your make-up to help you navigate different scenarios. For example, applying a darker blush or touching up your concealer can make you feel better prepared for the bar after a day in the office. In this way, make-up can support us as we go with the flow of the day.

4. It boosts confidence

The lipstick effect is the theory that people will forgo big luxuries for little ones like make-up during times of economic hardship. Historical studies have argued that women, in particular, do this to increase their attractiveness because supposedly, when you're broke, getting a man is a top priority. Thankfully, other studies have progressed with the times and have suggested another explanation for the lipstick effect. A tanking economy is stressful, especially if you internalise it and question your financial decisions. When we apply make-up to express ourselves, be creative and help us navigate different scenarios, it has been proven to boost our self-esteem.[49] So, of course, we lean on make-up as an easy pick-me-up during trying times.

Interestingly, research has revealed that make-up has an indirect effect on intelligence. A 2017 study called 'Does make-up make you feel smarter?' which monitored students' performance after an exam revealed that students who put on make-up received higher grades than those who did not. No, make-up is not a performance-enhancing drug. It simply increased the students' perceived beauty, which enhanced their self-confidence, leading to a 'better cognitive performance'.[50] Look good, feel good, be smart.

How to tell if your relationship with make-up is becoming unhealthy

Although make-up can have the positive impacts outlined above, when we start placing too much importance on cosmetics to help us shape external perceptions, it can have the opposite effect, undermining our mood and self-esteem.[51] One survey conducted by the Renfrew Centre found that nearly half of all female respondents 'have negative feelings when they don't wear make-up – describing themselves as unattractive, self-conscious and naked'.[52] This negative thought process is a recipe for disaster.

Your relationship with make-up might be unhealthy if the following statements are true for you.

- You can't bear to go a day or leave the house without it.
- You won't stop applying it even if it's causing you skin problems.
- You devalue your natural beauty compared to your beat face.
- People in your inner circle have never seen you without make-up.

Here are two things you can try when make-up stops being fun.

Change the content you're consuming

Step away from #beautytutorials and start looking at fresh faces. A 2019 study by Jasmine Fardouly and Ronald Rapee revealed that viewing #nomakeup selfies can spare you from experiencing the low mood and reduction in self-esteem that comes from being overly reliant on make-up.[53] It can also encourage you to go make-up-free more often.

Practise mirror meditation

One study asked women to stare at their bare faces in the mirror for an extended period over two weeks solely to be present with themselves. When the two weeks were over, they became less concerned with make-up and more comfortable in their own skin, and showed more self-compassion.[54]

As with your clothes, you should only wear make-up that feels right to you. When applying it, you should revel in the process and be cognisant of the impact it has on you. There's a fine line between make-up being good and being harmful. The same is true for cosmetic procedures.

New face, who dis?

Many people think it's paradoxical for cosmetic procedures to have the same upward trajectory as the self-love movement. If you genuinely love yourself, you should also love your supposed flaws, right? But could adjusting your appearance to help it become more in line with your ideal self also count as a form of self-love? It's a debate that exists beyond the scope of this book, and one that has scrambled more than a few heads (mine included). I'm aware that this topic is incredibly divisive, and even though I won't drill down into cosmetic procedures, the sheer popularity of them makes this a conversation worth having.

Cosmetic procedures have undergone their own kind of makeover. Going under the knife was once taboo, but now, with phrases like 'Zoom face' sidling into our lexicon, the days when a new nose would be waved off as the result of a procedure to fix a deviated septum are long gone. Roughly 27,000 cosmetic procedures were carried out in 2017 in the UK alone.[55] These days, many patients aren't even subject to a doctor's scalpel, as the popularity of non-surgical treatments is on the rise globally.[56]

Before you consider getting any work done, I would strongly advise you to ask yourself the following questions:

1. Is the price far too good to be true because the procedure is being done by a shady, unlicensed doctor in some remote 'hospital' with little to no mention of aftercare? (You would think this would go without saying, but at the time of writing, the TV show *Botched* is currently in its seventh season.)
2. What are your motivations for getting work done and where do they stem from?

3. How do you expect to feel after your procedure? Are your expectations realistic?

Making cosmetic decisions for the right reasons

Cardi B was right, fixing your teeth 'ain't cheap'. In 2020, I dropped £4,000 to get Invisalign treatments. So far, it's the most I have ever spent on something that serves purely cosmetic purposes. By no means did I *need* straight teeth. My teeth functioned as they should, despite me using them as a multipurpose tool to open crisp packets and pull corks out of wine bottles. I was often told that my crooked teeth weren't 'that noticeable'. They weren't bad enough for the NHS to give me braces when I was a teenager, no matter how much I begged. When J. Cole's 'Crooked Smile' came out, I can't lie and say I didn't consider whether my teeth were best left alone, but that feeling didn't last. So, I pulled the trigger.

Around the same time, I started to think about getting my lips done too. 'Nothing ridiculous,' I thought, 'just a touch plumper.' I even grappled with the ignorant belief that my small lips alongside my moderate posterior somehow diminished my Blackness. I believed that, just like my teeth, getting my lips done would make me feel better about myself, and that was reason enough to go under the needle. My desire for bigger lips began right around the time when I decided to promote more of my work in fashion psychology, which involved being more active on social media. Being more active on social media means consistently creating and editing content of yourself. It also leads you to follow a stream of funny, inspirational and beautiful people, either as a source of inspiration or for simple enjoyment. While social media has certainly brought joy and countless opportunities, it's not without its flaws.

Content creation involves editing, and boy, are we spoilt for choice. Editing tools and filters alike can do everything from removing a weird shadow on your picture to completely changing the structure of your face. When you constantly perceive yourself through a filtered lens, it can warp your perception of what you see in the mirror. Researchers and mental health professionals regularly warn us that filters can damage self-esteem, make you lose touch with reality and even trigger Body Dysmorphic Disorder[57] – a mental health condition where a person spends a lot of time worrying about flaws that are often unnoticeable to others.[58] At the same time, the endless scroll also breeds upward social comparison, and the results are nasty. In 2016, one study discovered a positive association between upward social comparison through social media and body image dissatisfaction in women.[59]

After reading into this, I assessed the amount of time I spent online and took a much-needed break. During this time, I realised that while my desire to straighten my teeth was internally motivated, my desire to enlarge my lips was externally motivated. Beyond it being something that I had wanted to do for a long time, getting Invisalign was a decision that felt incredibly personal to me. My crooked teeth were why I preferred to be seen with a sultry pout rather than a cheery smile. They stopped me from laughing as loud as I wanted, and niggled at my confidence. It was a feeling I couldn't self-love my way through. Upon realising this, I understood that I couldn't justify my desire for larger lips in the same way. When I stopped using filters for every picture, my lips didn't look as small anymore. I then realised that I hadn't even explored the hordes of liners, lipsticks and glosses available that offered a less invasive plumping effect.

The chief goal of both cosmetic procedures and make-up is to look good, and as you know, when you look good, you feel good – but you won't feel good if your motivations come from the wrong place. Research suggests that cosmetic procedures can only positively impact your self-esteem if your motivation for getting them done is internal, such as expressing your creativity (by turning into Picasso with your eyeliner brush) or having more agency over your appearance. When your motivations for getting something done are external, your mood and self-esteem will take a turn for the worse.[60]

When modifying your appearance, you should also consider what you think will happen afterwards. According to clinical psychologist Dr Deanna Hall, when people consistently go under the knife, they are never satisfied with their results. They seem hellbent on changing how they look because they overestimate the impact of the change. As Dr Hall told me, 'It's important to have realistic expectations. You'll likely be disappointed if you expect your life to drastically change after undergoing any cosmetic procedure.' As your relationship with your appearance changes, so too may your feelings towards cosmetic surgery. Before making such a permanent decision, it's important to make sure you've engaged in a sufficient amount of introspection to reduce the chances of you looking back and thinking, 'Why the hell did I do that?'

Hairology

'Hair is an important part of our identity. How we choose to wear it reflects how we want to be seen or perceived by the outside world.'

Vernon François

Your hair is no stranger to the mind–body connection. According to dermatologist Dr Flor Mayoral, your body 'takes a time-out from growing hair' following stressful periods like surgery or childbirth.[61] Outside of these stressful periods, your hair can be a powerful mood-booster if you consider it a way to connect and express your different sides.

For many people, hair is inextricably linked to identity. Whether you've had the same style since childhood or are constantly reinventing your look, hair can go a long way towards helping you express the identity you've forged for yourself and the one you choose to show the world. Having a good hair day is more important than you might think. A 2000 study commissioned by Procter & Gamble revealed that being dissatisfied with your hair can lead to increased self-criticism and social insecurities, and can even reduce your belief in your ability to achieve personal goals.[62] Whoever's side you took after 'the slap' at the 2022 Oscars (where actor Will Smith slapped comedian Chris Rock for making a joke related to Smith's wife Jada Pinkett-Smith's hair loss), most of us can agree on the fact that hair loss is an extremely delicate topic.[63]

When I spoke to celebrity hairstylist Veron François, who has worked with Serena Williams, Solange Knowles and Lupita Nyong'o, he stressed the importance of considering more than just how your hair looks:

A good hairstylist will always talk with their client about the role that hair plays in their life, whether they do or don't embrace their hair's true texture and the reasons around that. Understanding the client's needs, desires and expectations is crucial to achieving successful outcomes beyond the salon chair. There is always a bigger picture to be explored beyond the style itself, with something as personal and unique to each individual as their hair texture is.

There's a joke on Twitter that goes, 'When she dyes her head red, you've lost her.' It refers to how a drastic change to your hair can double as a rebirth, signifying the end of a difficult time and the beginning of a new you: one who won't put up with the same old nonsense. This is a premise that Vernon is familiar with.

It is not unusual for clients to have their hair done after a significant event in their life, like having a baby, following a break-up, or starting a new job. People say the effect is often a sense of feeling reinvigorated, and particularly that going short after having longer hair feels liberating. A change of any kind, small or dramatic, with the hair's cut, colour or style can be uplifting. Many women have told me that having their hair cut short has made them feel more confident, expressive and feminine.

The instant gratification that comes with making a drastic change to your hair can provide you with a much-needed sense of control when you feel helpless. It can be liberating to shed the image you once associated with a person or situation that didn't work out. However, we should proceed with caution. Taking things too far and ending up with a style or cut that you hate will only make things worse. According to psychotherapist Rebecca Newman, patience is everything. When speaking to *Dazed* magazine, she suggested that before sitting in the stylist's chair, you should ask yourself, 'If you are making the decision from an empowered place, a place of fear, or trying to use it as a synthetic means of internal change.'[64] Take time to consider your choice. Think carefully about how your new style will work in everyday life and if you'll make the effort to maintain it. That way, you can avoid a full-blown identity crisis.

Beauty Psychology tip

If you need to get a new perspective on life, changing up your hair might be a simple and effective way to do this – but please heed Vernon's warning and, for the love of God, 'Don't be tempted to cut or trim your own hair, even a small amount'.

Black hair

As Vernon says, 'hair can also have cultural, historical, social and geographical relevance', and I couldn't agree more. When I gave up the creamy crack (chemical hair straighteners) for good and started my natural hair journey, I felt like I was honouring my roots, both literally and figuratively. That was until my niece asked, 'Aunty, why do you always pull your hair back in one?' One question from this little six-year-old sent me into a tailspin. Why wasn't I letting my 4C coils fly freely? Why hadn't I put in more work to maintain my hair and discover new styles? But that's precisely what it is – work. Don't get me wrong, caring for your natural hair can be incredibly rewarding, but it's definitely not easy. I've done styles that have taken me four days to complete. That's not a misprint. *Days* is correct. I've spent a lot of energy hunting down the right brushes and conditioners to make detangling a less traumatic experience. Don't even get me started on the bonnets that go for walkies in the night, leaving you with a dry head and an oily pillow. And that's only half of it.

A 2018 report revealed that hair, specifically the maintenance, time and money that goes into its upkeep, acts as a socio-cultural barrier, preventing Black women from engaging in more physical activities.[65] I've wanted to take up swimming for a long time, but you can't simply jump in the pool when you're a Black woman. There are a lot of hair-related factors to consider to ensure you're in the best possible position to fully enjoy the experience. And sometimes, as the iconic Sweet Brown would say, 'Ain't nobody got time for that.' To top it off, Black people are still facing hair discrimination around the globe. A group of young Black UK activists called the Halo Collective challenged this issue when they launched the 'Halo Code' in 2020. The code is designed to prevent discrimination based on hairstyle or texture.

> Race-based hair discrimination has been illegal in the UK since the Equalities Act became law in 2010, yet it still happens all the time. For too long, Black people have been told that our hair textures and hairstyles are inappropriate, unattractive, and unprofessional. We've been suspended from school, held back in our careers, and made to feel inferior by racist policies and attitudes.[66]
>
> The Halo Collective

I'll never forget my mother having to produce a doctor's note to encourage my school to allow me to wear braids! It's wild she had to resort to that level of finessing to simply let me be me while trying to get an education. I'm thankful that my niece and nephew are less likely to face the same issues but, like many Black people, I have a lot of unlearning to do when it comes to my relationship with my hair. If you feel the same way, then start small. Start seeing wash days as less of a chore and more of an opportunity to take some necessary time out for yourself to really see your hair in all its bouncy glory. Utilise social media to explore new natural hair looks, but don't put yourself in a box. One of the things I love most about my hair is its versatility. I won't stop giving the people all kinds of braids, wigs and weaves. I'm even daydreaming about my upcoming style right now. I just need to make room for my 4C coils as well.

Now that you're equipped with all these insights into just how important your appearance is in shaping your mood and sense of self, don't let anyone make you feel guilty for spending those extra minutes in front of the mirror. Researchers from the Koirala Institute of Health Science revealed that failing to perform 'adequate cosmetic care of skin and hair can have a significant negative psychological impact'.[67] However, a high level of maintenance and the right products can only go so far. The difference between a good skin-and-hair day and a bad one has a lot to do with your mind – so consider that every time you stand before a mirror, products in hand. Going all out and being creative with your appearance comes with far too many benefits for you to ignore.

Key takeaways

★ The mind–body connection reveals that every mental state has an associated physiological response that impacts our overall health. This is one of the many reasons why it's important to tackle problems like stress head-on.

★ Psychodermatology was created to address the mind–body connection across three areas:
  ☆ how skin problems are created by emotional states
  ☆ how psychiatric problems manifest themselves via the skin
  ☆ how psychological issues occur as a result of skin problems

★ The five-step Beauty Psychology Routine allows you to incorporate psychodermatological practices into your daily life, allowing you to take care of your mind and skin at the same time.

★ For those who choose to wear it, make-up can help them express their creativity, have fun and navigate the day. The positive benefits are only applicable if you're internally motivated to wear make-up, not if you're wearing it in response to external pressures, or over-exaggerating the impact the application will have on your value. The same can be said for cosmetic procedures.

★ Making the decision to drastically change your hair can double as an act of self-control and a physical marker of a new chapter in life.

★ Hair is inextricably linked to identity, and this is particularly true for those who've historically faced hair discrimination, so it's important to be kind to yourself and considerate of others when discussing the topic of hair.

Conclusion

Unpicking the seams

'Buy less, choose well, make it last.'

Vivienne Westwood

When the legendary designer uttered these words in 2013, I feel like we collectively agreed this was the new goal. Sadly, there weren't a lot of detailed instructions about how to make it happen. It all starts with developing a better relationship with your clothes, and this comes from having an insight into their true significance. By this point, you should have a firm understanding that your clothes carry five powers:

1. The power to express and celebrate your identity
2. The power to control your external perceptions
3. The power to shift your behaviour
4. The power to help you embrace or change your mood
5. The power to help you evolve as a person

With this new-found knowledge – and, hopefully, new way of thinking – you have everything you need to embody Big Dress Energy. You can even retake the 'Big "Big Dress Energy" quiz' on page 6 to track your progress. The roles played by our clothes, accessories, skin, hair, cosmetics and every other part of our appearance in our everyday lives is often dismissed or not addressed in depth. By acknowledging their roles, we're providing ourselves with more tools for self-improvement. Beyond that, major concepts like sustainability, inclusivity and self-care don't really work without an appreciation of fashion psychology, because you need to understand how the mind works in order to have any hope of successfully promoting a major societal shift.

While taking in all of these lessons, I want you to remember that life is not static; it ebbs and flows. Cultural norms change, and the fashion industry with them. As such, your style will constantly evolve. Come back to this book as many times as you need to in order to stay on the right path and avoid losing yourself to a mound of clothes or to an image that's inconsistent with the real you.

I know from first-hand experience that life is too short to not look good and feel great while living it. In an effort to improve and love ourselves, we often engage in time-consuming, money-draining practices, when some of the tools for self-improvement are literally hanging two feet away from us in our wardrobes.

You can't simply dress your way into a new life because life isn't a makeover show hosted by the Fab Five (wouldn't that be great, though?!). Instead, you can arm yourself with the psychological know-how to craft a style you truly love – one that helps you navigate the stresses of daily life. With this book and a bit of willpower, you'll firmly set yourself on the path to buying less, choosing well and making your clothes last – word to Queen Viv.

Acknowledgements

This book wouldn't be possible without the support of my family and friends.

My mother, Wendy Forbes, and father, Desmond Bell, are the most supportive parents a girl could ask for. You've encouraged me every step of the way – even when I decided to do a random degree no one had ever heard of. My mother and late sister, Janelle, in particular practically forced me to keep pushing with fashion psychology when I was fretting about future job opportunities. Thank you for giving me the courage.

To my niece and nephew, Kaiden and Mia: your endless love and insane sense of humour have been a bright light in my most trying days.

To my literary agent, Lauren Gardner: you saw a book in me when I only saw a blog and not much else. I can't thank you enough for believing in me and sticking by me when I lost faith.

I literally harassed my besties, Alysha Yates, Holly Lord and Nicola Mouskis, for the best part of a year, going on and on about this book and they never got sick of me. I will forever cherish you ladies. Your support means everything. And to my darling family and friends who consistently gave me ideas and words of encouragement – Lisa O'Brien, Deanna Hall, Tessa O'Brien, Yola Timothy, Falanna Best, Kafelé O'Brien, Danté Best,

Claudine Bell, Lou Nylander, Selina Terrones-Shibuya, Jessica Berry, Lucia Papadopoulos and Nilam Atodaria – a major thank you as well.

I couldn't have made it this far, especially in the final months before my manuscript submission, without the practical support of my mentor and biggest cheerleader, Dr Aurore Bardey, and my right-hand woman, Maisie Allum. You ladies are constantly inspiring me to do better. To my agent Juanita Rosenior and editor Bernadette Marron, thank you for keeping me on track and helping me to produce my best work by reminding me to listen to my body and be myself.

And finally, to all the psychologists who've produced studies in this under-researched field; to everyone who lent me their voice for this book; to all my contributors; to everyone from the *Fashion is Psychology* community, from my new followers to those who have been with me since my days on Weebly: a sincere and heartfelt thank you!

Recommended reading

Banim, M., Green, E., and Guy, A. (2001). *Through the Wardrobe: Women's Relationships with their Clothes*. Berg.

Barber, A. (2021). *Consumed: The need for collective change; colonialism, climate change & consumerism*. Hachette UK.

de Castro, O. (2020). 'Loved Clothes Last'. *APRIA Journal*, 1(1), 111.

Elliot, A. J., Fairchild, M. D., and Franklin, A. (Eds.). (2015). *Handbook of Color Psychology*. Cambridge University Press.

Entwistle, J. (2015). *The Fashioned Body: Fashion, Dress and Social Theory*. John Wiley & Sons.

González, A. M., and Bovone, L. (Eds.). (2012). *Identities through Fashion: A Multidisciplinary Approach*. Berg.

Haller, K. (2019). *The Little Book of Colour: How to Use the Psychology of Colour to Transform Your Life*. Penguin UK.

Taylor, S. R. (2021). *The Body Is Not an Apology: The Power of Radical Self-love*. Berrett-Koehler Publishers.

Underhill, P. (2009). *Why We Buy: The Science of Shopping – Updated and Revised for the Internet, the Global Consumer, and Beyond*. Simon and Schuster.

References

Introduction: What on earth is fashion psychology?

1. Brus, J., Aebersold, H., Grueschow, M., Polania, R. (2012). 'Sources of confidence in value-based choice'. *Nature Communications*, 12 (1).

1: It's giving what it's supposed to

1. Guy, A., and Banim, M. (2000). 'Personal collections: Women's clothing use and identity'. *Journal of Gender Studies*, 9(3), 313–327.
2. Stone, G. P. (1962). 'Appearance and the Self'. In A. M. Rose (Ed.), *Human Behavior and Social Processes: An Interactionist Approach* (86–118). Houghton Mifflin.
3. Wilson, E. (1985). *Adorned in Dreams: Fashion and Modernity*. University of California Press.
4. Turner, J. C., Brown, R. J., and Tajfel, H. (1979). 'Social comparison and group interest in ingroup favouritism'. *European Journal of Social Psychology*, 9(2), 187–204.
5. Stone. 'Appearance and the Self'. In A. M. Rose (Ed.), *Human Behavior and Social Processes: An Interactionist Approach*.
6. Hart, A. (2013). *Why you need to dress like your boss*. The *Guardian*. Retrieved 11 January 2022, from www.theguardian.com.
7. Stephanie Newman, S. (2010). 'Why Your Teen Insists on Dressing Exactly Like Her Friends'. *Psychology Today*. Retrieved 20 February 2022 from www.psychologytoday.com.
8. Akdemir, N. (2018). 'Visible expression of social identity: The clothing and fashion'. *Gaziantep University Journal of Social Sciences*, 17(4), 1389–1397.
9. Tajfel, H. (1981). *Human Groups and Social Categories*. Cambridge University Press.
10. Mental Health Foundation. (2019). 'Body image report – Executive Summary'. Retrieved 20 February 2022 from www.mentalhealth.org.uk.
11. Bell, R., Cardello, A. and Schutz, H. (2005). 'Relationship between perceived clothing comfort and exam performance'. *Family and Consumer Sciences Research Journal*, 33, 308–320.
12. Kelly, E. (2019). 'Rose McGowan's infamous naked VMAs dress was a response to sexual assault'. *Metro*. Retrieved 20 February 2022 from metro.co.uk.
13. François, M. (2021). '"I felt violated by the demand to undress": three Muslim women on France's hostility to the hijab'. The *Guardian*. Retrieved 20 February 2022 from www.theguardian.com.
14. Lough, R., Ausloos, M., and Hudson, A. (2021). 'Hands off my hijab! Young Muslim women protest proposed French ban'. *Reuters*. Retrieved 20 February 2022 from www.reuters.com.

15. Fryberg, S. (2020). 'How Native American Team Names Distort Your Psychology'. Retrieved 3 May 2022, from https://www.politico.com/.
16. Blumer, H. (1969). 'Fashion: From class differentiation to collective selection'. *The Sociological Quarterly*, 10(3), 275–291.

2: Shh! Let the clothes do the talking

1. Willis, J., and Todorov, A. (2006). 'First Impressions: Making Up Your Mind After a 100-Ms Exposure to a Face'. *Psychological Science*, 17(7), 592–598.
2. Harris, M. and Bays, G. (1973). 'Altruism and sex roles'. *Psychological Reports*, 32, 1002.
3. Hamid, P. N. (1972). 'Some effects of dress cues on observational accuracy, a perceptual estimate, and impression formation'. *The Journal of Social Psychology*, 86(2), 279–289.
4. Gillath, O., Bahns, A. J., Ge, F., and Crandall, C. S. (2012). 'Shoes as a source of first impressions'. *Journal of Research in Personality*, 46(4), 423–430.
5. Gillath *et al.* 'Shoes as a source of first impressions'.
6. Craik, J. (2009). *Fashion: The Key Concepts*. Berg.
7. Molloy, J. T., and Potter, S. (1975). *Dress for Success*. Warner Books.
8. Bravata, D. M., Watts, S. A., Keefer, A. L., Madhusudhan, D. K., Taylor, K. T., Clark, D. M., Nelson, R. S., Cokley, K. O., and Hagg, H. K. (2020). 'Prevalence, Predictors, and Treatment of Impostor Syndrome: a Systematic Review'. *Journal of General Internal Medicine*, 35(4), 1252–1275.
9. Kwon, Y. H. (1991). 'The influence of the perception of mood and self-consciousness on the selection of clothing'. *Clothing and Textiles Research Journal*, 9(4), 41–46.
10. Kasperk, C., Helmboldt, A., Borcsok, I., Heuthe, S., Cloos, O., Niethard, F. and Ziegler, R. (1997). 'Skeletal site-dependent expression of the androgen receptor in human osteblastic cell populations'. *Calcified Tissue International*, 61, 464–473.
11. Molloy and Potter. *Dress for Success*.
12. McCarthy, M. (2017). 'A psychotherapeutic exploration of the impact of the therapist's clothing in the room'. Dublin Business School, School of Arts.
13. Mendes, W. and Kraus, M. (2014). 'Sartorial symbols of social class elicit class-consistent behavioral and physiological responses: A dyadic approach'. *Journal of Personality and Social Psychology*, 143.
14. Howlett, N., Pine, K., Orakçıoğlu, I. and Fletcher, B. (2013). 'The influence of clothing on first impressions: Rapid and positive responses to minor changes in male attire'. *Journal of Fashion Marketing and Management*, 17(1), 38–48.
15. Scherbaum, C. J., and Shepherd, D. H. (1987). 'Dressing for success: Effects of color and layering on perceptions of women in business'. *Sex Roles*, 16(7), 391–399.
16. Rucker, M., Taber, D., and Harrison, A. (1981). 'The effect of clothing variation on first impression of female job applicants: What to wear when'. *Social Behavior and Personality*, 9(1), 54–64.
17. Carney, D. R., Hall, J. A. and LeBeau, L. S. (2005). 'Beliefs about the nonverbal expression of social power'. *Journal of Nonverbal Behavior*, 29, 105–123.
18. Carney, D. R., Cuddy, A. J. C. and Yap, A. J. (2010). 'Power Posing: Brief Nonverbal Displays Affect Neuroendocrine Levels and Risk Tolerance'. *Psychological Science*, 21(10), 1363–1368.
19. Huang, L., Galinsky, A., Gruenfeld, D. and Guillory, L. (2011). 'Powerful Postures Versus Powerful Roles'. *Psychological Science*, 22, 95–102.
20. Paek, S. L. (1986). 'Effect of Garment Style on the Perception of Personal Traits'. *Clothing and Textiles Research Journal*, 5(1), 10–16. 2
21. Jacob, C., Guéguen, N. and Delfosse, C. (2012). 'She Wore Something in Her Hair: The Effect of Ornamentation on Tipping'. *Journal of Hospitality Marketing & Management*, 21, 414–420.

22. European Science Foundation. (2009). 'Tiny Ancient Shells – 80,000 Years Old – Point To Earliest Fashion Trend. *ScienceDaily*. Retrieved 18 February 2022 from www.sciencedaily.com.
23. Bilefsky, D. (March 2017). 'British Woman's Revolt Against High Heels Becomes a Cause in Parliament'. *New York Times*. www.nytimes.com.
24. McCann, S. J. H. (2001). 'Height, Societal Threat, and the Victory Margin in Presidential Elections (1824–1992)'. *Psychological Reports*, 88(3), 741–742. 1
25. Duguid, M. M., and Goncalo, J. A. (2012). 'Living Large: The Powerful Overestimate Their Own Height'. *Psychological Science*, 23(1), 36–40.
26. Guéguen, N., Stefan, J. and Renault, Q. (2016). 'Judgments towards women wearing high heels: a forced-choice evaluation'. *Fashion and Textiles*, 3(6).
27. Springer Science and Business Media. (November 2014). 'High heels may enhance a man's instinct to be helpful'. *ScienceDaily*. Retrieved 19 February 2022 from www.sciencedaily.com.
28. Doob, A. N. and Gross, A. E. (1968). 'Status of frustrator as an inhibitor of horn-honking responses'. *The Journal of Social Psychology*, 76(2), 213–218.
29. Nelissen, R. M. A. and Meijers, M. H. C. (2011). 'Social benefits of luxury brands as costly signals of wealth and status'. *Evolution and Human Behaviour*, 32(5), 343–355.
30. Swami, V., Chamorro-Premuzic, T. and Furnham, A. (2009). 'Faking it: Personality and individual difference predictors of willingness to buy counterfeit goods'. *Journal of Socio-Economics*, 38, 820–825.
31. Gino, F. and Norton, M. (2010). The Counterfeit Self: The Deceptive Costs of Faking It'. *Psychological Science*, 21. 712–20.
32. Gray, K., Schmitt, P., Strohminger, N., and Kassam, K. (2014). 'The Science of Style: In Fashion, Colors Should Match Only Moderately'. *PloS ONE*, 9(7).
33. Morris, T. L., Gorham, J., Cohen, S. H., and Huffman, D. (1996). 'Fashion in the classroom: Effects of attire on student perceptions of instructors in college classes'. *Communication Education*, 45(2), 135–148.
34. Rahman, O. (2012). 'The influence of visual and tactile inputs on denim jeans evaluation'. *International Journal of Design*, 6(1), 11–25.

3: Embrace the rainbow

1. Itten, J., and Veres, P. (1961). *The Art of Color: The Subjective Experience and Objective Rationale of Color*. John Wiley & Sons.
2. Stitch Fix UK. (2021). www.stitchfix.co.uk.
3. Clarke, A., and Miller, D. 'Fashion and Anxiety'. UCL Anthropology. Retrieved 30 March 2022 from https://www.ucl.ac.uk/anthropology.
4. Patra, R. (2016). 'To Dye For: A history of natural and synthetic dyes'. Patra. Retrieved 30 March 2022 from blog.patra.com.
5. Science Learning Hub. 'Colours of light'. Retrieved 30 March 2022 from www.sciencelearn.org.nz.
6. Elliot, A. J., Fairchild, M. D., and Franklin, A. (Eds.). (2015). *Handbook of Color Psychology*. Cambridge University Press.
7. Palmer, S. E., and Schloss, K. B. (2010). 'An ecological valence theory of human color preference'. *Proceedings of the National Academy of Sciences of the United States of America*, 107(19), 8877–8882.
8. Deutscher, G. (2010). *Through the Language Glass: Why the World Looks Different in Other Languages*. Metropolitan Books.
9. Naz, K., and Helen, H. (2004). 'Color-emotion Associations: Past Experiences and personal preference'. AIC 2004 Color and Paints, Interim Meeting of the International Color Association, Proceedings.5.

10. Ishii, K., Numazaki, M., and Tado'oka, Y. (2019). 'The effect of pink/blue clothing on implicit and explicit gender-related self-cognition and attitudes among men'. *Japanese Psychological Research*, 61(2), 123–132.
11. Elliot, Fairchild, and Franklin. *Handbook of Color Psychology.*
12. Yokosawa *et al.* Under review.
13. Stitch Fix UK.
14. Hill, R., and Barton, R. (2005). 'Red enhances human performance in contests'. *Nature* 435, 293.
15. Attrill, M., Gresty, K., Hill, R. and Barton, R. (2008). 'Red shirt colour is associated with long-term team success in English football'. *Journal of Sports Sciences*, 26, 577–82.
16. Hill and Barton. 'Red enhances human performance in contests'.
17. Ilie, A., Ioan, S., Zagrean, L., and Moldovan, M. (2008). Better to be red than blue in virtual competition. *Cyberpsychology & Behavior*, 11(3), 375–377.
18. Hill and Barton. 'Red enhances human performance in contests'.
19. Wiedemann, D., Burt, M., Hill, R. and Barton, R. (2015). 'Red clothing increases perceived dominance, aggression and anger'. *Biology Letters*, 11(5).
20. Elliot, A. J., Niesta Kayser, D., Greitemeyer, T., Lichtenfeld, S., Gramzow, R. H., Maier, M. A., and Liu, H. (2010). 'Red, rank, and romance in women viewing men'. *Journal of Experimental Psychology: General*, 139(3), 399.
21. Guéguen, N. (2012). 'Does red lipstick really attract men? An evaluation in a bar'. *International Journal of Psychological Studies*, 4(2), 206.
22. Tham, D. S. Y., Sowden, P. T., Grandison, A., *et al.* (2020). 'A systematic investigation of conceptual color associations'. *Journal of Experimental Psychology: General*, 149(7), 1311–1332.
23. Costa, M., Frumento, S., Nese, M., Predieri, I. (2018). 'Interior color and psychological functioning in a university residence hall'. *Frontiers in Psychology*, 9, 1580.
24. Patil, D. (2012). 'Coloring consumer's psychology using different shades the role of perception of colours by consumers in consumer decision-making process: A micro-study of select departmental stores in Mumbai City, India'. *Journal of Business and Management Research*, 7(1), 60–73.
25. Labrecque, L. I., and Milne, G. R. (2012). 'Exciting red and competent blue: the importance of color in marketing'. *Journal of the Academy of Marketing Science*, 40, 711–727.
26. O'Connor, Z. (2011). 'Colour psychology and colour therapy: Caveat emptor'. *Color Research & Application*, 36(3), 229–234.
27. Maglaty, J. (2011). 'When Did Girls Start Wearing Pink?'. *Smithsonian Magazine*. www.smithsonianmag.com.
28. Labrecque and Milne. 'Exciting red and competent blue'.
29. Koller, V. (2008). 'Not just a colour': pink as a gender and sexuality marker in visual communication. *Visual Communication*, 7(4), 395–423.
30. Mammarella, N., Di Domenico, A., Palumbo, R. and Fairfield, B. (2016). 'When green is positive and red is negative: Aging and the influence of color on emotional memories'. *Psychology and Aging*, 31(8), 914–926.
31. Schnoor, J. L. 'The benefits of being green'. (2012). *Environmental Science & Technology*, 46(21), 11487.
32. Clay, R. A. (2001). 'Green is good for you'. *Monitor on Psychology*, 32(4), 40.
33. Lichtenfeld, S., Elliot, A. J., Maier, M. A., and Pekrun, R. (2012). 'Fertile green'. *Personality and Social Psychology Bulletin*, 38(6), 784–797.
34. Mammarella *et al.*, 'When green is positive, and red is negative'.
35. Labrecque and Milne, 'Exciting red and competent blue'.
36. Murray, D. C. and Deabler, H. L. (1957). 'Colors and mood-tones'. *Journal of Applied Psychology*, 41(5), 279–83.

37. Gazibegovic, N. (2018). 'How do different colours affect your mood, judgement and physiology?'. *Scientific Scribbles*, www.blogs.unimelb.edu.au.
38. CareerBuilder. (2013). 'New CareerBuilder Study Looks at Best and Worst Colors to Wear in a Job Interview' (press release). www.press.careerbuilder.com.
39. Mehta, R. and Zhu, R. J. (2009). 'Blue or Red? Exploring the Effect of Color on Cognitive Task Performances'. *Science* 323(5918), 1226–9.
40. Labrecque and Milne. 'Exciting red and competent blue'.
41. *Symbols of the Women's Suffrage Movement (U.S. National Park Service)*. Nps.gov. (2022). Retrieved 25 January 2022 from https://www.nps.gov.
42. BioMed Central. (2010). 'Depressed people feel more gray than blue'. www.sciencedaily.com.
43. Clarke, T. and Costall, A. (2008). 'The emotional connotations of color: A qualitative investigation'. *Color Research & Application*, 33, 406–410.
44. Markovic, Z. (2014). 'Colour as an Element of the Creativity in Education of Design'. *Open Journal of Social Sciences*, 2(05), 76.
45. Anderson, E., Cowen, T., Dawes, R. M., Crocker, D. A., Elster, J., Etzioni, A. and Weston, S. C. (1998). *Economics, Ethics, and Public Policy*. Rowman & Littlefield.
46. Vrij, A., Pannell, H., and Ost, J. (2005). 'The influence of social pressure and black clothing on crime judgements'. *Psychology, Crime & Law*, 11(3), 265–274.
47. G. F. Smith. (2017). 'The world's favourite colour report'. www.gfsmith.com.
48. Labrecque and Milne. 'Exciting red and competent blue'.
49. Uebayashi, K., Tado'oka, Y., Ishii, K., and Murata, K. (2016). 'The effect of black or white clothing on self-perception of morality'. *Japanese Journal of Experimental Social Psychology*, 55(2), 130–138.
50. Cherry, K. (2021). 'The color psychology of white'. Verywell Mind. www.verywellmind.com.
51. Damhorst, M. and Reed, A. (1986). 'Clothing color value and facial expression: Effects of evaluations of female job applicants.' *Social Behavior and Personality: An International Journal*, 14(1), 89–98.
52. Haller, Karen. (2019). *The Little Book of Colour*. Penguin Life.

4: New look, who dis?

1. Adam, H., and Galinsky, A. D. (2012). 'Enclothed cognition'. *Journal of Experimental Social Psychology*, 48(4), 918–925.
2. Cherry, K. (2019). 'What Role Do Schemas Play in the Learning Process?'. Verywell Mind. Retrieved 19 February 2022 from www.verywellmind.com.
3. Lammers, J., Stoker, J. I., Rink, F. and Galinsky, A. D. (2016). 'To Have Control Over or to Be Free From Others? The Desire for Power Reflects a Need for Autonomy'. *Personality and Social Psychology Bulletin*, 42(4), 498–512.
4. Slepian, M. L., Ferber, S. N., Gold, J. M., and Rutchick, A. M. (2015). 'The Cognitive Consequences of Formal Clothing'. *Social Psychological and Personality Science*, 6(6), 661–668.
5. Hannover, B., and Kühnen, U. (2002). '"The Clothing Makes the Self" Via Knowledge Activation 1'. *Journal of Applied Social Psychology*, 32(12), 2513–2525.
6. Ellis, D. A., and Jenkins, R. (2015). 'Watch-wearing as a marker of conscientiousness'. *PeerJ*, 3, e1210.
7. Davies, G., Lam, M., Harris, S.E. *et al.*(2018). 'Study of 300,486 individuals identifies 148 independent genetic loci influencing general cognitive function'. *Nature Communications*, 9, 2098.
8. Hartley, J. (2015). 'How your clothes can affect – and improve – your mood'. *Stuff*. Retrieved 27 February 2022 from www.stuff.co.nz.
9. Elliot, A. J. and Maier, M. A. (2014). 'Color Psychology: Effects of Perceiving Color on Psychological Functioning in Humans'. *Annual Review of Psychology,* 65:1, 95–120.

10. Wang, Y. and Roedder John, D. 'Louis Vuitton and Conservatism: How Luxury Consumption Influences Political Attitudes'. Marketing Department, Carlson School of Management, University of Minnesota.
11. Fredrickson, B., Roberts, T., Noll, S., Quinn, D. and Twenge, J. (1998). 'That Swimsuit Becomes You: Sex Differences in Self-Objectification, Restrained Eating, and Math Performance'. *Journal of Personality and Social Psychology*, 75, 269–84.
12. Felig, R., Jordan, J., Shepard, S., Courtney, E., Goldenberg, J. and Roberts, T. (2021). 'When looking "hot" means not feeling cold: Evidence that self-objectification inhibits feelings of being cold'. *British Journal of Social Psychology*, 61(2), 455–70.
13. Marchant, J. L. and Frith, C. D. (2009). 'Social Cognition'. Squire, L. R. (Ed.). Encyclopedia of Neuroscience, Academic Press, 2009, pp 27–30, www.sciencedirect.com
14. Adam and Galinsky. Enclothed cognition'.

5: Wearapy

1. Young, S. (2019). *Women Choose Outfits Based on How Clothes Make Them Feel While Men Care More About What Others Think*. The *Independent*. Retrieved 19 February 2022 from https://www.independent.co.uk.
2. Healthline Medical Network. (2019). 'Gamma Aminobutyric Acid: Uses and Side Effects of GABA Supplement'. Healthline. Retrieved 30 March 2022 from www.healthline.com.
3. Young, S. *Women Choose Outfits Based On How Clothes Make Them Feel While Men Care More About What Others Think*.
4. Groov. 'Know your brain: A quick guide to serotonin'. www.groovnow.com.
5. Kumar, S. (2019). 'What We Wear Represent Our Personalities and Feelings'. *Entrepreneur*. Retrieved 28 January 2022 from www.entrepreneur.com.
6. Kwon, Y. H. (1991). 'The Influence of the Perception of Mood and Self-Consciousness on the Selection of Clothing'. *Clothing and Textiles Research Journal*, 9(4), 41–46.
7. Hartley, J. (2015). 'Fashion and mood: How clothes affect your emotions'. Smh.com.au. Retrieved 28 February 2022 from www.smh.com.au.
8. Fletcher, B. (2016). *Doing Something Different for Anxiety and Depression*. Psychology Today. Retrieved 25 February 2022, from https://www.psychologytoday.com/
9. Fletcher, B. and Pine, K. J. (2012). *Flex: do something different*. University of Hertfordshire Press.
10. Fernández-Espejo, E. (2000). 'Cómo funciona el nucleus accumbens?' [How does the nucleus accumbens function?]. *Revue Neurologique*, 30(9), 845–9. Spanish.
11. 'Pre-frontal cortex'. Science Direct. From: *Textbook of Natural Medicine (Fifth Edition)*, 2020. www.sciencedirect.com.
12. Chaney, D. (2014). '"Look!! I'M Not the Same Person!": The Role of Clothing in Consumers Escapism'. *NA: Advances in Consumer Research*, 42, 427.
13. Moody, W. and Sinha, P. (2010). 'An Exploratory study: Relationships between Trying on Clothing, Mood, Emotion, Personality and Clothing Preference'. *Journal of Fashion Marketing and Management*, 14(1), 161–179.
14. 'Cultural Assimilation'. (2021). Wikipedia. wikipedia.org.
15. 'Cultural Appropriation'. (2018). *Oxford Dictionary*.
16. 'Self-Concept'. Lexico. Retrieved 21 February 2022 from lexico.com.
17. Cheema, S. (2021). 'Why am I uncomfortable in my ethnic dress?'. *Fashion is Psychology*. Retrieved 27 February 2022 from fashionispsychology.com.
18. Bhui, K., Khatib, Y., Viner, R., *et al*. (2008). 'Cultural identity, clothing and common mental disorder: a prospective school-based study of white British and Bangladeshi adolescents'. *Journal of Epidemiology & Community Health*, 62, 435–441.
19. Grandin, T. (1992). 'Calming effects of deep touch pressure in patients with autistic disorder,

college students, and animals'. *Journal of Child and Adolescent Psychopharmacology.* Spring, 2(1), 63–72.

20. San Francisco State University. (2011). 'Seeking happiness? Remember the good times, forget the regrets'. ScienceDaily. Retrieved 13 March 2022 from www.sciencedaily.com.

21. Zhou, X., Wildschut, T., Sedikides, C., Chen, X., and Vingerhoets, A. J. J. M. (2012). 'Heartwarming memories: Nostalgia maintains physiological comfort'. *Emotion*, 12(4), 678–684.

22. Oostermeijer, M. (2021). 'Can fashion help with grief?'. 1 Granary. Retrieved 27 February 2022 from 1granary.com.

23. Kim, J., Kim, J. E., and Johnson, K. K. (2010). 'The customer-salesperson relationship and sales effectiveness in luxury fashion stores: the role of self-monitoring'. *Journal of Global Fashion Marketing*, 1(4), 230–239.

24. Levy, L. (2014). 'Women's Expressions of Grief, from Mourning Clothes to Memory Books'. JSTOR Daily. Retrieved 27 February 2022 from daily.jstor.org.

6: Well, you can't be naked

1. Entwistle, J. (2015). *The Fashioned Body: Fashion, dress and social theory*. John Wiley & Sons.

2. Entwistle. *The Fashioned Body*.

3. Labat, K., and DeLong, M. (1990). 'Body cathexis and satisfaction with fit of apparel'. *Clothing and Textiles Research Journal*, 8, 43–48.

4. Slade, P. D. (1994). 'What is body image?'. *Behaviour Research and Therapy*, 32(5), 497–502.

5. Ralph-Nearman, C., Arevian, A., Puhl, M., Kumar, R., Villaroman, D., Suthana, N., Feusner, J. and Khalsa, S. (2019). 'A Novel Mobile Tool (Somatomap) to Assess Body Image Perception Pilot Tested With Fashion Models and Nonmodels: Cross-Sectional Study'. *JMIR Mental Health*, 6 (10).

6. Labat and DeLong. 'Body cathexis and satisfaction with fit of apparel'.

7. Fish, I. (2020). 'Majority of shoppers' uncomfortable' with trying on clothes'. *Drapers*. Retrieved 22 February 2022 from www.drapersonline.com.

8. Wang, J., Wang, H., Gaskin, J. and Hawk, S. (2017). 'The Mediating Roles of Upward Social Comparison and Self-esteem and the Moderating Role of Social Comparison Orientation in the Association between Social Networking Site Usage and Subjective Well-Being'. *Frontiers in Psychology*, 8, 771.

9. University of Chicago Press Journals. (2011). 'Consumer self-esteem while shopping: Maybe good-looking clerks shouldn't wear the store brands?' ScienceDaily. Retrieved 22 February 2022 from www.sciencedaily.com.

10. Kinley, T. R. (2010). 'The effect of clothing size on self-esteem and body image'. *Family and Consumer Sciences Research Journal*, 38(3), 317–332.

11. Forbes-Bell, S. (2017). 'How Size Labels For Clothing Can Really Affect You'. *Marie Claire*. Retrieved 22 February 2022 from www.marieclaire.co.uk.

12. Taylor, S. R. (2021). *The Body is Not an Apology: The Power of Radical Self-love*. Berrett-Koehler Publishers.

13. Schurrer, M. (2019). 'How to Reframe Negative Self-Talk Around Body Image'. HealthyPlace. Retrieved 22 February 2022 from www.healthyplace.com.

14. Patrick, V. M. and Hagtvedt, H. (2012). '"I Don't" versus "I Can't": When Empowered Refusal Motivates Goal-Directed Behavior'. *Journal of Consumer Research*, 39(2). 371–381.

15. Howlett, Pine, *et al*. 'The influence of clothing on first impressions'.

16. Price, B. R., and Pettijohn, T. F. (2006). 'The effect of ballet dance attire on body and self-perceptions of female dancers'. *Social Behavior and Personality: An International Journal*, 34(8), 991–998.

17. Grogan, S., Gill, S., Brownbridge, K., Kilgariff, S., and Whalley, A. (2013). 'Dress fit and

body image: A thematic analysis of women's accounts during and after trying on dresses'. *Body Image*, 10(3), 380–388.

18. Chattaraman, V., and Rudd, N. A. (2006). 'Preferences for Aesthetic Attributes in Clothing as a Function of Body Image, Body Cathexis and Body Size'. *Clothing and Textiles Research Journal*, 24(1), 46–61.

19. Brathwaite, K. N. and DeAndrea, D. C. (2022). 'BoPopriation: How self-promotion and corporate commodification can undermine the body positivity (BoPo) movement on Instagram'. *Communication Monographs*, 89(1), 25–46.

20. Braithwaite and DeAndrea. 'BoPopriation'.

21. Oltuski, R. (2017). 'Please Stop Telling Me to Love My Body: Embracing body neutrality'. Man Repeller. Retrieved 10 January 2022 from www.manrepeller.com.

22. Grogan, Gill, *et al*. 'Dress fit and body image'.

23. Feldon, L. (2007). *Does This Make Me Look Fat?: The Definitive Rules for Dressing Thin for Every Height, Size, and Shape*. Villard.

24. UserTesting. (2019). '7 Gestalt Principles of Visual Perception: Cognitive Psychology for UX.' www.usertesting.com/blog.

25. Forbes-Bell. (2020). 'The Perfect Dress for Your Body Type According to Psychology Style & Beauty.' *Fashion Is Psychology*. fashionispsychology.com.

26. Helmholtz, H. V. (1925). 'Treatise on psychological optics'. *Optical Society of America*, 3, 482.

27. Thompson, P., and Mikellidou, K. (2011). 'Applying Helmholtz illusion to fashion: Horizontal stripes won't make you look fatter'. *i-Perception*, 2, 69–76.

28. Koutsoumpis, A., Economou, E., and van der Burg, E. (2021). 'Helmholtz Versus Haute Couture: How Horizontal Stripes and Dark Clothes Make You Look Thinner'. *Perception*, 50(9), 741–756.

29. Thompson and Mikellidou. 'Applying Helmholtz illusion to fashion'.

30. Entwistle. *The Fashioned Body*.

31. Reddy, S., and Otieno, R. (2013). 'Relationship between body image and clothing perceptions: Among women aged 18–55 years in the UK'. *International Journal of Arts and Commerce*, 2(5), 40–49.

32. Ashley, B. (2020). 'What happened to plus-size?'. *Vogue Business*. Retrieved 24 February 2022 from www.voguebusiness.com.

33. Afterpay US data, February 2022.

34. Smith, P. (2022). 'UK: plus size clothing market size 2012–2022'. Statista. Retrieved 24 February 2022 from www.statista.com.

35. Downing Peters, L. (2014). 'You Are What You Wear: How Plus-Size Fashion Figures in Fat Identity Formation'. *Fashion Theory*, 18:1, 45–71.

36. Elias, T., Appiah, O., and Gong, L. (2011). 'Effects of strength of ethnic identity and product presenter race on black consumer attitudes: A multiple-group model approach'. *Journal of Interactive Advertising*, 11(2), 13–29.

37. Bernabe, A. (2022). 'Texas A&M basketball coach pushes back after criticism for wearing pink pants on the court'. ABC13 Houston. Retrieved 23 February 2022 from abc13.com.

38. Aitkenhead, D. (2017). 'Former Vogue editor Alexandra Shulman: "I find the idea that there was a posh cabal offensive"'. The *Guardian*. Retrieved 24 February 2020 from www.theguardian.com.

39. Forbes-Bell, S., Bardey, A. C., and Fagan, P. (2020). 'Testing the effect of consumer-model racial congruency on consumer behavior'. *International Journal of Market Research*, 62(5), 599–614.

40. Bower, A. B. (2001). 'Highly attractive models in advertising and the women who loathe them: The implications of negative affect for spokesperson effectiveness'. *Journal of Advertising*, 30(3), 51–63.

41. Heiser, C. (2021). 'Report: Fashion Month Spring 2022 Is Officially the Most Racially Diverse Season Ever as Size, Age and Gender Representation See Slight Gains'. The Fashion Spot. Retrieved 24 February 2022 from thefashionspot.com.
42. Department for Work & Pensions. (2021). 'Family Resources Survey'. Department for Work & Pensions. Retrieved from www.gov.uk.
43. Friis Dam, R., and Siang, T. (2021). 'What is Design Thinking and Why Is It So Popular?'. The Interaction Design Foundation. Retrieved 24 February 2022 from www.interaction-design.org.
44. Radin, S. (2021). 'The Fashion Industry Is Ableist, and Stylist Stephanie Thomas Created a System to Change That'. InStyle. Retrieved 28 March 2022 from www.instyle.com.
45. McKinley, H. (2021). 'Disability Stylist Stephanie Thomas Is Done Asking the Fashion Industry For Favours'. POPSUGAR Fashion UK. Retrieved 24 February 2022 from www.popsugar.co.uk.

7: Hanger management

1. Cwerner, S. B. (2001). 'Clothes at Rest: Elements for a Sociology of the Wardrobe'. *Fashion Theory*, 5(1), 79–92.
2. Lamb, J. M., and Kallal, M. J. (1992). 'A conceptual framework for apparel design'. *Clothing and Textiles Research Journal*, 10(2), 42–47.
3. North London Waste Authority. (2020). 'Join the Swish and Style Clothes Swap Revolution'. www.nlwa.gov.uk.
4. Lloyd, K. and Pennington, W. (2020). 'Towards a theory of minimalism and wellbeing'. *International Journal of Applied Positive Psychology*, 5, 121–136.
5. Crisell, H. (2017). 'Do you spend £1042 on clothes each year? New research reveals the average Brit's shopping habits'. The *Telegraph*. Retrieved 27 February 2022 from www.telegraph.co.uk.
6. Bunzeck, N. and Duzel, E. (2006). 'Absolute Coding of Stimulus Novelty in the Human Substantia Nigra/VTA'. *Neuron*, 51, 369–79.
7. Wittmann, B. C., Daw, N. D., Seymour, B., and Dolan, R. J. (2008). 'Striatal activity underlies novelty-based choice in humans'. *Neuron*, 58(6), 967–973.
8. Gregson, N. and Beale, V. (2004). 'Wardrobe matter: The sorting, displacement and circulation of women's clothing'. *Geoforum*, 35, 689–700.
9. Cwerner, 'Clothes at Rest'.
10. ClosetMaid. www.closetmaid.ca.
11. Daily Mail Reporter. (2016). 'The average woman has 103 ITEMS in her closet'. *Mail Online*. (2016). Retrieved 30 March 2022 from www.dailymail.co.uk.
12. Cwerner. 'Clothes at Rest'.
13. Sanocki, T., and Sulman, N. (2011). 'Color Relations Increase the Capacity of Visual Short-Term Memory'. *Perception*, 40(6), 635–648.
14. Loewenstein, G. and Adler, D. (1995). 'A Bias in the Prediction of Tastes'. *The Economic Journal*, 105(431), 929–937.
15. Clothes Aid. 'Facts on clothes recycling'. www.clothesaid.co.uk.
16. North London Waste Authority. Censuswide survey of 1,510 general respondents aged 16–40. December 2020.
17. Greater Good Science Center at UC Berkeley. (2018). 'The Science of Generosity'. John Templeton Foundation. Retrieved from ggsc.berkeley.edu.

8: Get in loser, we're going shopping

1. Stibel, J. (2018). 'Mind blown? Yes, there is proof that too much choice overwhelms your brain'. *USA Today*. Retrieved 27 February 2022 from eu.usatoday.com.

2. Sirgy, M. J. (1982). 'Self-concept in consumer behavior: A critical review'. *Journal of Consumer Research*, 9(3), 287–300.
3. Caldwell, C., and Hibbert, S. A. (1999). 'Play that one again: The effect of music tempo on consumer behaviour in a restaurant'. *European Advances in Consumer Research*, 4, 58–62.
4. Jang, J. Y., Baek, E. and Choo, H. J. (2018). 'Managing the visual environment of a fashion store: Effects of visual complexity and order on sensation-seeking consumers'. *International Journal of Retail & Distribution Management*, 46(2), 210–226.
5. Cialdini, R. (2001). 'Principles of Persuasion'. Arizona State University, eBrand Media Publication.
6. Orji, R., Mandryk, R. and Vassileva, J. (2015). 'Gender, Age, and Responsiveness to Cialdini's Persuasion Strategies'. *Persuasive Technology*. Springer.
7. University of Chicago Press Journals. (2012). 'Retail therapy: Shopping to cope with future challenges'. ScienceDaily. Retrieved 20 February 2022 from www.sciencedaily.com.
8. Weisbaum, H. (2016). *What's up, America? Why do we keep buying things we never wear?*. NBC News. Retrieved 13 January 2022, from https://www.nbcnews.com.
9. Maslow, A. H. (1943). 'A theory of human motivation'. *Psychological Review*, 50(4), 370.
10. Belk, R. W. (1988). 'Possessions and the extended self'. *Journal of Consumer Research*, 15(2), 139–168.
11. Koch, J., Frommeyer, B., and Schewe, G. (2020). 'Online shopping motives during the COVID-19 pandemic – lessons from the crisis'. *Sustainability*, 12(24), 10247.
12. *British Medical Journal*. (2011). 'Frequent shopping prolongs life, study suggests'. ScienceDaily. Retrieved 19 February 2022 from www.sciencedaily.com.
13. Johnson, K. and Kang, M. (2010). 'Let's Shop'. *Journal of Global Fashion Marketing*, 1.
14. Kröner, S., Krimer, L. S. , Lewis, D. A. and Barrionuevo, G. (2007). 'Dopamine increases inhibition in the monkey dorsolateral prefrontal cortex through cell type-specific modulation of interneurons'. *Cerebral Cortex*, 17(5), 1020–32.
15. Kahneman, D., and Tversky, A. (1979). 'On the interpretation of intuitive probability: A reply to Jonathan Cohen'. *Cognition*, 7(4), 409–11.
16. Hippocratic Post. (2020). 'The Pandemic and shopping addiction'. Retrieved 30 March 2022 from www.hippocraticpost.com.
17. Sol, B. (2021). *How to Save It: Fix Your Finances*. Penguin Publishing.
18. Brigham Young University. (2013). 'Shopping in high heels could curb overspending'. ScienceDaily. Retrieved 20 February 2022 from www.sciencedaily.com.
19. Chavan, S., Deshmukh, J., and Singh, B. (2017). 'Role of mindfulness, belief in personal control, gratitude on happiness among college students'. *Indian Journal of Health & Wellbeing*, 8(10).
20. Sporn, J., and Tuttle, S. (2018). '5 Surprising Findings About How People Actually Buy Clothes and Shoes'. *Harvard Business Review*. Retrieved 20 February 2022 from hbr.org.
21. Crockett, Z. (2019). 'Drunk shopping is a $45B industry. Here's what people are buying'. *The Hustle*. Retrieved 20 February 2022 from thehustle.co.
22. Boston College. (2010). 'Anatomy of a shopping spree: Pretty things make us buy more'. ScienceDaily. Retrieved 19 February 2022 from www.sciencedaily.com.
23. Russo, M. A., Santarelli, D. M., and O'Rourke, D. (2017). 'The physiological effects of slow breathing in the healthy human'. *Breathe*, 13(4), 298–309.
24. Underhill, P. (2009). *Why We Buy: The Science of Shopping – Updated and revised for the Internet, the global consumer, and beyond*. Simon and Schuster.
25. University of Chicago Press Journals. (2010). 'Rose-colored glasses have many shades: Shopping decisions and emotions'. ScienceDaily. Retrieved 20 February 2022 from www.sciencedaily.com.

9: Beauty psychology

1. Zhang, Y., Kong, F., Zhong, Y., and Kou, H. (2014). 'Personality manipulations: Do they modulate facial attractiveness ratings?'. *Personality and Individual Differences*, 70, 80–4.
2. University of Minnesota. 'What Is the Mind–Body Connection?' Taking Charge of Your Health & Wellbeing. Retrieved 25 February 2022 from www.takingcharge.csh.umn.edu.
3. American Heart Association News. (2020). 'Chronic stress can cause heart trouble'. Retrieved 25 February 2022 from www.heart.org.
4. University of Minnesota, 'What Is the Mind–Body Connection?' .
5. França, K., Chacon, A., Ledon, J., Savas, J. and Nouri, K. (2013). 'Pyschodermatology: a trip through history'. *Anais Brasileiros de Dermatologia*, 88(5), 842–843.
6. Barr, K. (2019). 'An Integrative Dermatologist Explains Why Your Skin & Mental Health Are So Connected'. Mind Body Green. Retrieved 25 February 2022 from www.mindbodygreen.com.
7. Ayodele, D. (2021). *Black Skin: The Definitive Skincare Guide*. HQ.
8. Happiness makes you beautiful Oxytocin, and cortisol interaction affects skin ageing. The 31st IFSCC Congress 2020 Yokohama, Poster-64, 1357–1364.
9. Nguyen, A. V., and Soulika, A. M. (2019). 'The Dynamics of the Skin's Immune System'. *International Journal of Molecular Sciences*, 20(8), 1811.
10. Barr, K. (2019). 'An Integrative Dermatologist Explains Why Your Skin & Mental Health Are So Connected'. Mind Body Green. Retrieved 25 February 2022 from www.mindbodygreen.com.
11. American Academy of Dermatology. (2007). 'Feeling Stressed? How Your Skin, Hair And Nails Can Show It'. ScienceDaily. Retrieved 9 February 2022 from www.sciencedaily.com.
12. Garg, A., Chren, M. M., Sands, L. P., Matsui, M. S., Marenus, K. D., Feingold, K. R. and Elias, P. M. (2001). 'Psychological stress perturbs epidermal permeability barrier homeostasis: implications for the pathogenesis of stress-associated skin disorders'. *Archives of Dermatology*, 137(1), 53–9.
13. Manoylov, M. (2020). 'Does stress cause wrinkles? Yes, it can speed up skin aging'. Insider. Retrieved 25 February 2022 from www.insider.com.
14. Vaughan, S. (2016). 'Hidden meanings behind the lines and wrinkles on your face'. Qi Medicine Acupuncture Melbourne Fertility and Pregnancy. Retrieved 25 February 2022, from qimedicine.com.au.
15. Hess, U., Adams, Jr R. B., Simard, A., *et al.* (2012). 'Smiling and sad wrinkles: Age-related changes in the face and the perception of emotions and intentions'. *Journal of Experimental Social Psychology*, 48(6), 1377–1380.
16. Statista. (2022). 'Value of the global anti-aging market 2020–2026'. Statista Research Department. Retrieved from www.statista.com.
17. Uvence. (2020). 'Is 30 the new 40?'. Uvence: A Revolutionary Treatment. Retrieved 25 February 2022 from uvence.co.
18. NHS. (2018). '10 stress busters'. www.nhs.uk.
19. Piedmont Healthcare. '4 Reasons Friends and Family are Good for Health'. Retrieved 28 March 2022 from www.piedmont.org.
20. Chin, B., Slutsky, J., Raye, J., and Creswell, J. D. (2019). 'Mindfulness training reduces stress at work: A randomized controlled trial'. *Mindfulness*, 10(4), 627–38.
21. NHS, '10 stress busters'.
22. Varvogli, L., and Darviri, C. (2011). 'Stress management techniques: Evidence-based procedures that reduce stress and promote health'. *Health Science Journal*, 5(2), 74.
23. Diamond, E. (2021). 'Does Stress Result in Oily Skin?' Psychreg. Retrieved 25 February 2022 from www.psychreg.org.
24. Fama, J. 'What is Skin Picking Disorder?'. International OCD Foundation. Retrieved 25 February 2022 from iocdf.org.

25. Brown, E. (2022). 'This Is Why Popping Your Pimples Feels So Satisfying'. *Vice*. Retrieved 25 February 2022 from www.vice.com.
26. Watson, K. (2019). 'How to Pop a Pimple: Safety, Side Effects, and More'. Healthline. Retrieved 25 February 2022 from www.healthline.com.
27. Columbia University Irving Medical Center. (2021). 'Stress can turn hair grey – and it's reversible, researchers find'. ScienceDaily. Retrieved 15 February 2022 from www.sciencedaily.com.
28. Barankin, B., and DeKoven, J. (2002). 'Psychosocial effect of common skin diseases'. *Canadian Family Physician*, 48, 712–716.
29. Mayo Clinic. (2021). 'Rosacea – Symptoms and causes'. Retrieved 25 February 2022 from www.mayoclinic.org.
30. Clay, R. (2015). 'The link between skin and psychology'. American Psychological Association. Retrieved 25 February 2022 from www.apa.org.
31. Barankin and DeKoven. 'Psychosocial effect of common skin diseases'.
32. Sakamoto, K., Lochhead, H., Maibach, H., and Yamashita, Y. (Eds.). (2017). *Cosmetic Science and Technology: Theoretical Principles and Applications*. Elsevier.
33. Musial, F., and Weiss, T. (2014). 'The Healing Power of Touch: The Specificity of the "Unspecific" Effects of Massage'. *Complementary Medicine Research*, 21(5), 282–283.
34. Sakamoto, Lochhead, *et al. Cosmetic Science and Technology*.
35. Kao (2018). 'Confirmation of Relationship between "Comfort" from Touching the Skin during Skin Care and the Change in Cerebral Blood Flow'. Kao. Retrieved 23 February 2022 from www.kao.com.
36. Kao (2018). 'Research on Skin Care with a Focus on Stimulation that Creates Pleasant Feelings'. Kao. Retrieved 23 February 2022 from www.kao.com.
37. Owens, A. (2021). 'Oxytocin: What It Is, How It Makes You Feel & Why It Matters'. Psycom. Retrieved 23 February 2022 from www.psycom.net.
38. Clay. 'The link between skin and psychology'.
39. Clay. 'The link between skin and psychology'.
40. Farshi, S. (2011). 'Comparative study of therapeutic effects of 20% azelaic acid and hydroquinone 4% cream in the treatment of melasma'. *Journal of Cosmetic Dermatology*, 10(4), 282–287.
41. Zhang, L. Chen, W., Liu, M., Ou, Y., Xu, E. and Hu, P. (2021). 'Light makeup decreases receivers' negative emotional experience'. *Scientific Reports*, 11, 23802.
42. Robertson, J. M., and Kingsley, B. E. (2021). 'Behind the Façade: Motivations for Cosmetic Usage by Women'. *SAGE Open*, 11(4).
43. Statista. (2022). 'Global value of the cosmetics market 2018–2025'. Retrieved from www.statista.com.
44. Korichi, R., Pelle-de-Queral, D., Gazano, G. and Aubert, A. (2008). 'Why women use makeup: implication of psychological traits in makeup functions'. *Journal of Cosmetic Science*, 59(2), 127–37.
45. Tran, A., Rosales, R. and Copes, L. (2020). 'Paint a Better Mood? Effects of Makeup Use on YouTube Beauty Influencers' Self-Esteem'. *SAGE Open*, 10(2).
46. Tran, Rosales and Copes. 'Paint a Better Mood?'.
47. Tran, Rosales and Copes. 'Paint a Better Mood?'.
48. Apaolaza, V., Hartmann, P., Diehl, S. and Terlutter, R. (2011). 'Women's satisfaction with cosmetic brands: The role of dissatisfaction and hedonic brand benefits'. *African Journal of Business Management*, 5.
49. Robertson and Kingsley. 'Behind the Façade'.
50. Palumbo, R., Fairfield, B., Mammarella, N. and Di Domenico, A. (2017). 'Does makeup make you feel smarter? The 'lipstick effect' extended to academic achievement'. *Cogent Psychology*, 4, 1.

51. Robertson and Kingsley. 'Behind the Façade'.
52. Renfrew Centre, 2012. 'New Survey Results Indicate There's More to Makeup Use Than Meets the Eye'. PR Newswire. Retrieved 15 February 2022 from /www.prnewswire.com.
53. Wang, J., Wang, H. *et al* 'The Mediating Roles of Upward Social Comparison and Self-esteem'.
54. Well, T., *et al*. (2016). 'The Benefits of Mirror Meditation'. Paper presented at the American Psychological Association Convention in Denver, CO.
55. Statista. (2022). 'Plastic surgeons in the United Kingdom (UK) in 2021, by staff grade'. www.statista.com.
56. Alliance Cosmetic Center. 'Plastic Surgery Trends Around the World'. Retrieved 25 February 2022 from www.alliancecosmeticcenter.com.
57. Boston Medical Center. (2018). 'A new reality for beauty standards: How selfies and filters affect body image'. ScienceDaily. Retrieved 6 February 2022 from www.sciencedaily.com.
58. NHS. 'Body dysmorphia'. www.nhs.uk.
59. Fardouly, J., Diedrichs, P. C., Vartanian, L. R. and Halliwell, E. (2015). 'Social comparisons on social media: The impact of Facebook on young women's body image concerns and mood'. *Body Image*, 13, 38–45.
60. Robertson and Kingsley. 'Behind the Façade'.
61. American Academy of Dermatology. 'Feeling Stressed?'
62. Scarponi, D. (2000). 'Yale study ponders psychology of all those bad hair days'. Journal Times. Retrieved 25 February 2022 from journaltimes.com.
63. Tsioulcas, A. (2022). 'Jada Pinkett Smith's hair loss, noted at the Oscars, is a struggle for many women'. NPR. Retrieved 30 March 2022 from www.npr.org.
64. Radin, S. (2019). 'We asked a psychologist and hairdresser why haircuts are so emotional'. *Dazed*. Retrieved 25 February 2022 from www.dazeddigital.com.
65. Joseph, R. P., Coe, K., Ainsworth, B. E., Hooker, S. P., Mathis, L., and Keller, C. (2018). 'Hair As a Barrier to Physical Activity among African American Women: A Qualitative Exploration'. *Frontiers in Public Health*, 5, 367.
66. Bakar, F. (2021). 'Finally, There's Hope That Hair Discrimination Could Be Made Illegal'. HuffPost UK. Retrieved 25 February 2022 from www.huffingtonpost.co.uk.
67. Marahatta, S., Singh A. and Pyakurel P. (2021). 'Self-cosmetic care during the COVID-19 pandemic and its psychological impacts: Facts behind the closed doors'. *Journal of Cosmetic Dermatology*, 20(10), 3093–7.